In Defense of
Sovereignty

In Defense of
Sovereignty

Protecting the Oneida Nation's
Inherent Right to Self-Determination

Rebecca M. Webster

With contributions by James R. Bittorf,
William Gollnick, Frederick E. Hoxie, Arlinda F. Locklear,
and James W. Oberly

Foreword by Richard Monette

THE UNIVERSITY OF WISCONSIN PRESS

publication supported by a grant from
The Community Foundation for Greater New Haven
as part of the Urban Haven Project

publication of this book has been made possible, in part, through
support from the Anonymous Fund of the College of Letters and Science
at the University of Wisconsin–Madison

The University of Wisconsin Press
728 State Street, Suite 443
Madison, Wisconsin 53706
uwpress.wisc.edu

Printed in the United States of America
This book may be available in a digital edition.

Library of Congress Cataloging-in-Publication Data

Names: Webster, Rebecca M., author.
Title: In defense of sovereignty : protecting the Oneida Nation's inherent
right to self-determination / Rebecca M. Webster ; with contributions by
James R. Bittorf [and 4 others] ; foreword by Richard Monette.
Description: Madison, Wisconsin : The University of Wisconsin Press, [2023] |
Includes bibliographical references and index.
Identifiers: LCCN 2022022453 | ISBN 9780299340605 (hardcover)
Subjects: LCSH: Oneida Indians—Wisconsin—Government relations. |
Oneida Nation—History. | Oneida Reservation (Wis.)
Classification: LCC E99.O45 W423 2023 | DDC 977.5004/975543—
dc23/eng/20220708
LC record available at https://lccn.loc.gov/2022022453

ISBN 9780299340643 (pbk.)

Contents

Illustrations

Foreword

RICHARD MONETTE

The book you are holding offers an engaging glimpse of the legal history of the Oneida Nation, an Indian tribe surrounded by the American State of Wisconsin. A stark story of pride, oppression, pain, and aspiration fills every crease in its pages. While *In Defense of Sovereignty* is uniquely Oneida's story, the book paints a broad-brush canvas of general tribal sovereignty, especially the three prerequisite components of international norms of sovereignty: 1) territorial integrity, 2) a distinct peoples, and 3) recognition by neighboring sovereigns. The U.S. Constitution prohibits Congress from forming "a state within a state" because the Founders knew full well the impracticability, if not impossibility, of having one sovereign's territory and citizenry surrounded by another's, a configuration that would challenge any relationship based on mutual recognition. The story of the Oneida Nation and the State of Wisconsin illustrates precisely what the Founders knew from the outset.

Rebecca Webster, the book's primary author, compiles a sweeping history as well as legal and political minutiae, all bundled like Oneida corn and braided like sweetgrass and sage. Webster brings several other authors along for the journey: historians, ethnographers, lawyers, and statesmen, each with their own unique perspective, each ably adding to a cogent story of the modern Oneida Nation. American historian James Oberly sets the stage by giving an expert rendition accessible to apprentice eyes of perhaps the two most complex parcels of recent Oneida history: the parallel emigration of competing Oneida factions from today's New

York and the resulting dissonant relationships with the United States and each other, especially over the acquisition of land in the western Great Lakes region. Ethnohistorian Fred Hoxie's chapter on "Allotment" provides as clear of an explanation of that inhumane policy period as any extant writing, but more importantly Hoxie elucidates allotment's peculiar and lasting carnage on the Oneida people, setting the stage for the book's core legal history. *In Defense of Sovereignty*'s persistent lawyering segues nicely in the clear voice of Arlinda Locklear in a chapter written with Oneida Nation attorney James Bittorf on allotment's nagging legal legacy. My favorite chapter, by Oneida statesman Bill Gollnick, adds a bluntly honest take, squinting through all the history, law, and policy with a modern Native lens unevenly honed by America's unforgiving cities and the grassroots activism of reservation life.

Make no mistake, this collection's crown jewel rests atop the bookend writings of its principal author Becky Webster who, almost defensively and apologetically, centers her voice on the land and among the people of the Oneida reservation. She opens the book with a humble rendition of Oneida culture and cosmology, from the Origin Story to the Great Law, illuminating the stage for Oneida teachings on relations and balance. Her own rendition of the Oneida story begins with a set of twins—the very personification of relation and balance in human terms, nicely illustrating her ultimate objective for future Oneida and non-Oneida children: "I believe they can accept others with open minds and that others will accept them."

Webster need not apologize, of course, as her contribution to the book illustrates above all else that culture comes from the dirt, that the relation between the dirt and those who live upon it dictates indigenous cosmology, a worldview best understood and explained by those who have lived it, then and now. Reservation life, where those who beget Oneida knowledge also live by it, informs her perspective, her thinking, and her words. As unbending as that can sound, especially to those who are not of that same dirt, Webster ends with a resounding note of hope, steeped in the teachings of relations and balance: "Our one constant is the need to do all we can so our future generations can not only continue to survive, but continue to thrive—and to do so on our own terms in ways that make sense for us as Oneida people. . . . The reservation is our home even though we may not all physically reside here. Speaking for those of us that do live here, I leave you with words fashioned from Henry 'Duke' Doxtator: We are Oneida Indians living on the reservation."

In Defense of Sovereignty's grand dispute over sovereignty and dominion between America and Oneida plays out on the stage of the small and generally inconsequential Village of Hobart and the Oneida Nation's annual Apple Festival, of all things. The resulting legal battles have been anything but inconsequential for the Oneida Nation, emerging as zoning disputes, condemnation proceedings, restrictive covenants, unauthorized taxes, and land use permits. True to form, in defending sovereignty, the story of the Oneida Nation and the Village of Hobart is one of territorial integrity, of distinct peoples, and mutual political recognition between neighbors. Centering the "territorial integrity" prong of sovereignty, Webster writes: "I currently reside on the Oneida reservation and have resided there most of my life." Centering the "distinct peoples" prong of sovereignty, she resolutely declares: "I am an enrolled citizen of the Oneida Nation." Centering on sovereignty's recognition prong, like her recent ancestors, she is "determined to win recognition for their past treaty relationship and to restore what they viewed as their historic alliance with the United States."

Intentionally or not, Webster and company offer a landscape rich with scholarly fodder beyond the Oneida story, its historical and legal detail providing finer shades and subtler nuances than are normally found in doctrinal law journals. *In Defense of Sovereignty* highlights the complexity of wending American law with indigenous worldviews. The cultural pretext of Webster's first chapter requires us to see relations in both directions in order to discern the proper balance. In referring to herself as an "enrolled citizen", Webster will and should cajole academic questions like: are there enrolled members who are *not* citizens and are there *un*enrolled citizens? Can citizenship only be based on relations with a territory? Or can citizenship be based only on relations with a historical people, in utter disregard of territory? *In Defense of Sovereignty* also offers examples of citizenship tied to territory and citizenship not tied to territory, examples of overlapping citizenries where perhaps there should be none, and examples of exclusive citizenries where some measure of counterbalance could prevail. Most importantly, *In Defense of Sovereignty* offers a rich opportunity to see them all in one compelling story.

Under the colonizer's legal narrative, native territory has become mere property and citizenry has become detached from territory. However, one is not a citizen of mere property; rather, one is a citizen of a territory. Thus, while allotment resulted in a huge loss of Oneida "land", what do we mean by that: a loss of territory or a loss of property? America, in subjugating Indian tribes, insists on referring to Native lands as mere property. Meanwhile, those pushing back on that subjugation have, perhaps necessarily, played the hand dealt them, unfortunately adopting the colonizer's lexicon, and in the process, perhaps unwittingly, reifying the colonizer's narrative. Start with the ubiquitous phrase "on the reservation"—one does not live "on" North Dakota or on California; one lives "in" them, so why is "on" the reservation accurate or acceptable?

The State of Wisconsin surrounds the Oneida reservation; the Oneida reservation surrounds the Village of Hobart. Is the Oneida Nation a mere aggregation of property within the state of Wisconsin? Is the Village of Hobart merely an aggregation of property within the territory of the Oneida Nation? By discerning the right relations and proper balance between them, Hobart's legal and political posturing come into clear relief, like the fabled elephant standing on an anthill whining about being outnumbered.

If the Oneida Nation held mere property without dominion over territory, how has the Village of Hobart, which merely acquired that Oneida property, come to be an incorporated polity with governance over territory? Is it possible that the Village of Hobart should be deemed incorporated under the laws of the Oneida Nation, acting merely as an aggregated constituency and property with home rule under the authority of the Oneida Nation? Will that require the Oneida Nation to act as a sovereign and issue a corporate charter to the Village? Will that require the Oneida Nation to extend citizenship to residents of Hobart, perhaps simply limited to Village matters? This is the Federal Indian Law which those who live there, as citizens, living in the cultural soil, will surely face in the not too distant future.

Beyond the scholarly, this book, *In Defense of Sovereignty*, provides a highly readable account of a complex legal history for all ages and should find itself offered both in "brick-and-mortar" libraries of old and online in the drop-down menu category of necessary readings for high-school- and college-aged students who take America's history seriously.

In Defense of
Sovereignty

Prologue

REBECCA M. WEBSTER

The Oneida people's story begins with né· thóne? tsyowehtau waekwa-tuhuntsyayʌ·tane (of the time it started when we received the earth).[1] A time before human beings walked on this earth. Part of our story describes a set of twins and their role in creation. Tehaluhyawá·ku (he holds the sky) went about creating plants and animals.[2] Shawíhskla (flint) was jealous of his brother's creations and tried to copy him. When Tehaluhyawá·ku created a bird, Shawíhskla also tried to make a bird, but his creation didn't quite come out as planned and he ended up creating a bat.

When Tehaluhyawá·ku started the process to create human beings, Shawíhskla watched him and rushed to create a human being himself. He copied his brother and stood up his creation, but it didn't have life yet. He asked Tehaluhyawá·ku for help. Tehaluhyawá·ku was reluctant because he didn't quite understand himself how he brought life to his own creations. Eventually, Tehaluhyawá·ku said he would help his brother. So, Tehaluhyawá·ku breathed life into Shawíhskla's creation. However, the being acted in a way that Shawíhskla manifested it to be. The being was an ape. Shawíhskla was upset that Tehaluhyawá·ku didn't give the being more than just his breath.

Shawíhskla was angry and decided that he should be in control of everything, even Tehaluhyawá·ku's creations. Tehaluhyawá·ku told Shaw-íhskla that they should be satisfied with the way things were and go about that way. Shawíhskla was not satisfied and decided to challenge

Tehaluhyawá·ku. The first challenge was a lacrosse game. It ended in a tie. The second challenge was a peachstone game. It also ended in a tie. The third game was hand-to-hand combat. Whoever survived would be in control of all things.

As they stood there waiting for the fight, Tehaluhyawá·ku was standing by a broken branch on the ground that was decayed and not strong. He thought about grabbing that stick to defend himself. Shawíhskla was standing by a pair of deer antlers on the ground. He thought about grabbing the antlers to kill his brother. When the fight started, they went into each other's mind and saw each other's intentions and choice of weapon. As the fight was about to begin, they switched their choice of weapon. Tehaluhyawá·ku grabbed the antlers to defend himself, and Shawíhskla grabbed the stick to kill his brother.

Because Tehaluhyawá·ku was in Shawíhskla's mind, he came away with the capacity to do something bad. During the fight, Tehaluhyawá·ku grazed his brother in the head with the antlers and knocked him out. While Shawíhskla was unconscious, Tehaluhyawá·ku went from one end of the earth to the other and divided it into day and night. Tehaluhyawá·ku decided there would be no winner and loser to the challenges. Rather, each would have creations on both sides of day and night, with most of Tehaluhyawá·ku's creations being active during the day and most of Shawíhskla's creations being active during the night.

After Tehaluhyawá·ku split the world into day and night, he continued with his effort to create human beings. Tehaluhyawá·ku formed the being from the soil of the earth. Then he took his own blood and put it into the being. Then he took his breath and breathed life into the being. Then he took a piece of his mind and placed that into the being so that it should always have a way of thinking of the things that he had given it. When Tehaluhyawá·ku created human beings, he intended us to treat each other with love and compassion. At this point in the creation story, after Tehaluhyawá·ku created human beings, we refer to him as Shukwaya?tísu (he made our bodies).

Many generations before European contact, the people were engulfed in a very dark time where warriors were going from village to village, causing death and destruction. This concerned Shukwaya?tísu because this is not how he intended human beings to treat one another. Never did he envision that his creation would carry on in such a manner. In response, he sent the Peacemaker to deliver a message of how human beings should be treating one another.[3] This message would be known as Kayanlásla?ko·wa (great matters).[4] The foundation of this message changes with time and different speakers. The version I am most familiar with sets forth three main governing principles: kanikuliyo/skana (peace of mind), kanolunkwatsla (love), and katsastʌnsla (power).

"Kanikuliyo/skana" has two meanings, both related to peace. The first is the peace that will settle everywhere around us when people stop killing each other because Shukwaya?tísu never intended human beings to treat one another this way. The second is the peace within ourselves, the stillness that we can create in our own minds. We often cannot control what happens around us, but we can control how we respond to it. "Kanolunkwatsla" means we should love each other and treat one another with compassion because we are all related. Even if we come from different nations or speak different languages, we should treat one another like family.

"Katsastʌnsla" refers to the power of the nations united in their efforts to become a single force. Our power is that we will join hands and survive as a group, as a single family and that the faces yet to be born, the future generations, will be able to continue on in this way. "Katsastʌnsla" also refers to the power of our minds. It is up to us how we control that power and utilize it. We can use it for good or we can use it for things that are not necessarily good. This connects back to the creation story when the twins fought. Tehaluhyawá·ku gained the ability to do harm by entering his brother's mind. When he later created human beings, he intended for us to be good, but we have the capacity to do things that are not good. We need to be mindful of how powerful our thinking can be and make an effort to choose to do good.

In bringing this message to the people, the Peacemaker helped establish a structure to organize the clans and tribal nations through diverse responsibilities and community participation. He brought together the Mohawk, Oneida, Onondaga, Cayuga, and Seneca people under one government, the Yukwanuhsyu·ní (we all build a house).[5]

The Peacemaker knew he couldn't force anyone to accept that message. He afforded the opportunity for people to understand it, and it was up to them whether to take hold of it and embrace it. Fortunately, all the people throughout this new confederacy embraced the message. When they agreed to accept the message, the Peacemaker had the people uproot a great white pine tree. In the hole left behind, the Peacemaker instructed the people to cast away the weapons they had used against one another. These weapons included literal weapons of war and combat as well as figurative weapons people had used against one another including the things they had said to one another. The people cast all those things in the hole. The Peacemaker then explained that the tributaries that ran below the earth would carry these things away. The future generations would never know what they had done to one another, and so they could henceforth live in a peaceful state of mind. The people then stood the tree back up so that the people could find the concepts the Peacemaker had left in the shade of the tree.

Fast-forward in time through colonization, assimilation, and removal. The Oneida people in Wisconsin, like other Yukwanuhsyu·ní communities, now find ourselves with two sets of "governments." The first is our original government the Peacemaker helped us establish, which currently serves to keep our language, culture, history, and ceremonies alive. The second is our elected, reorganized government formed pursuant to the Indian Reorganization Act of 1934. This second government is the Oneida Nation. Like many people in our community, I attend both our traditional ceremonies and Oneida Nation government meetings. While they may seem to be two separate universes, it is still the Oneida people that attend both. Whether consciously or subconsciously, our history shows how we have consistently carried with us the Peacemaker's message of kanikuliyo/skana, kanolunkwatsla, and katsastʌnsla.

Even in instances where the Oneida Nation is involved with intergovernmental conflicts challenging the Nation's ability to govern itself and its land, the Oneida people take the high road. We take the lessons from Tehaluhyawá·ku and Shawíhskla as they battled for control. Tehaluhyawá·ku wanted things to remain as they are where both brothers went about their activities in peace. Shawíhskla wanted to be in control of all creation, even the beings Tehaluhyawá·ku brought to life. When they entered the final contest for control, Tehaluhyawá·ku entered the fight with the intention of defending himself. Shawíhskla entered the fight with the intention of killing his brother.

Our stories, especially the story of né· thóne? tsyowehtau waekwatuhuntsyayʌ·tane and the Kayanláslaʔko·wa, are more than stories. They are more than folklore. They are more than metaphors. They are intended to remind us to be thankful for the world around us and our reciprocal responsibilities to all of creation. They are also intended to provoke thought, teach us lessons, serve as our moral compass, and guide our behaviors. They are set in place to help ensure that the faces yet to be born can come into a world full of kanikuliyo/skana, kanolunkwatsla, and katsastʌnsla.

Notes

1. Also referred to as our creation story. There are many versions of our creation story. I am sharing portions of the version I am familiar with.

2. Tehaluhyawá·ku is also referred to as Okwiláse (flint).

3. We do not use the Peacemaker's given name in casual conversation. There are certain times where it is acceptable to use his name.

4. In English, it is often referred to as the Great Law of Peace. Like the creation story, there are different versions of the Kayanláslaʔko·wa. I am sharing the version I am most familiar with.

5. Each nation has its own language and has different ways to describe itself and our collective nations. A few decades ago, when the people were getting ready to go to the Geneva Conference, the chiefs met to talk about how they were going to present themselves. Since the Onondaga are the central fire, they decided to use the Onondaga word "Haudenosaunee" (people who build the house). Previously referred to as Iroquois, Iroquois Confederacy, League of the Iroquois, or Six Nations. ("Six Nations" refers to the five nations mentioned as well as the Tuscarora, who migrated from North Carolina in 1722.)

Introduction

This Will Be Our Legacy

REBECCA M. WEBSTER

The Oneida Nation is a thriving community with a rich culture and history. The Oneida reservation is home to tribal citizens as well as non-tribal citizens. In addition to the Oneida Nation, the reservation is host to five municipal and two county governments: Town of Oneida, Village of Hobart, Town of Pittsfield, Village of Ashwaubenon, City of Green Bay, Outagamie County, and Brown County (see fig. 1). The Oneida Nation, individual tribal citizens, nontribal citizens, churches, schools, and nonprofits, as well as the federal government, state government, and local governments, own land on the reservation (see fig. 2). This mix of citizenship, ownership, and different layers of government can lead to a confusing jurisdictional landscape where it is not always obvious which government should handle a particular situation.

In order to make sense of the jurisdictional pattern, it is important to understand the history of the Oneida reservation. In the early 1820s, the federal government removed the Oneida people from New York to what would later become the State of Wisconsin. The federal government established the Oneida reservation in 1838, ten years before Wisconsin became a state. Since making this new place home, the Oneida people continued to suffer from various federal assimilationist policies. Encroaching neighbors helped push federal, state, and local policies to keep the Oneida people and our government disempowered. Despite

8

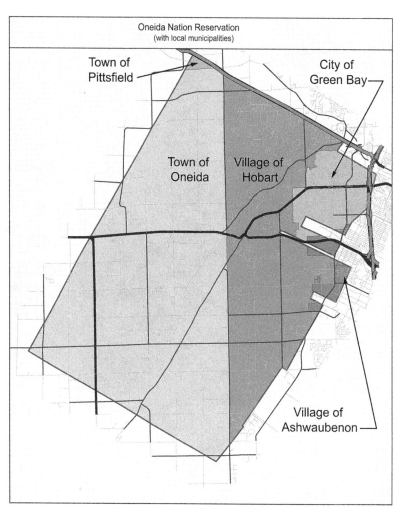

Map showing the five municipal governments located on the Oneida
Reservation: Town of Oneida, Town of Pittsfield, Village of Hobart, Village
of Ashwaubenon, and City of Green Bay. The Town of Oneida is located in
Outagamie County. The rest of the municipalities are located in Brown
County. Map provided by the Oneida Nation Geographic Land Information
Systems.

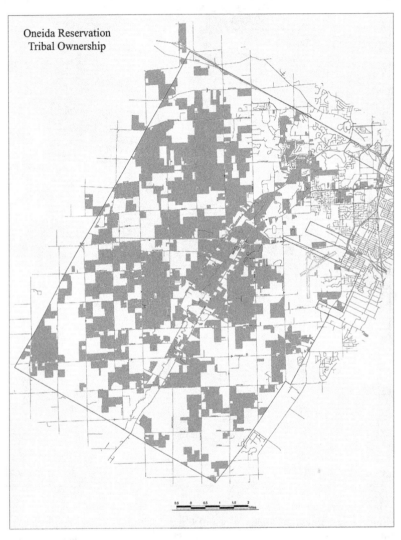

Map of the Oneida Reservation showing lands owned by the Oneida Nation. Map provided by the Oneida Nation Geographic Land Information Systems.

the circumstances, the Oneida Nation has repeatedly placed a priority on rebuilding our land base and reacquiring land lost through assimilationist federal Indian policies.

This book takes us through the Oneida Nation's history in order to properly frame the most recent conflicts arising, in part, because of the complex jurisdictional landscape on the Oneida reservation. However, where other governments have found ways to work through these issues, one municipal government would rather see the Oneida Nation wiped off the map than attempt to find ways to work together. The Village of Hobart launched a seventeen-year campaign involving a series of disputes, which ended up in litigation between the Nation and the Village. All of the lawsuits center on the Village's efforts to force the Nation to comply with Village authority. What follows are some talking points the Oneida Nation used to help inform citizens about the overarching themes of these lawsuits. They provide high-level summaries of the issues discussed in this book. This list summarizes the Village's theories:

- Oneida reservation does not exist.
- The Village has jurisdiction over fee land.
- The Nation is not properly organized under 1934 Indian Reorganization Act.
- The Nation did not exist until it was fraudulently recreated in 1937.
- Secretary of the Interior cannot take land into trust for the Nation.
- Federal Indian law should be changed in favor of state and municipal governments.

The goals of the Oneida Nation are to:

- Defend the Oneida reservation
- Protect trust land
- Support the authority of the federal Bureau of Indian Affairs (BIA) to take land into trust
- Challenge the Village's repeated assertions of authority
- Explore ways to minimize impacts to Tribal Citizens

We conclude that:

- Good governance is possible only with positive government-to-government relations. We need a clear understanding of one another's roles, responsibilities, and jurisdiction, and we need to respect each government's right to exist and exercise its jurisdiction.
- Some governments may seek to use litigation to change existing federal Indian laws and policies to disestablish tribal governments and Indian reservations. This approach ensures that our limited resources will continue to be directed to litigation.

Too often, the media and local governments control the narrative. While academic studies strive for unbiased observations of the world around us, my goal in this book is to provide some insider context to information that is readily available to the public, including court decisions, oral arguments, and newspaper articles. I am an enrolled citizen of the Oneida Nation. I currently reside on the Oneida reservation and have resided there most of my life, mostly on the portion of the reservation that the Village of Hobart occupies. I also served my Nation for thirteen years as an attorney on the negotiation team working on securing intergovernmental agreements with surrounding local governments. And I served on the litigation team when those intergovernmental relationships turned sour, mostly with the Village of Hobart. Those lawsuits are the focus of this book.

In writing this book, I was able to recruit others to add their voices to this story. These individuals served in various capacities to assist the Nation during the litigation process. Frederick E. Hoxie and James W. Oberly are two well-respected historians who prepared affidavits and expert reports for the Nation during litigation. Their respective chapters lay out a thorough and concise history supported by the voluminous written record. William Gollnick, an Oneida Nation citizen, is now retired after a lengthy career in a number of areas within the Oneida Nation, most notably as the chief of staff. He was the lead negotiator for our intergovernmental agreements. His chapter focuses on the history of the Oneida people through the eyes of an Oneida citizen. He was in the thick of the relatively recent history that led to the ultimate break-down of intergovernmental relations between the Nation and the Village. James R. Bittorf is the deputy chief counsel for the Oneida Law Office. He was the lead in-house attorney for these lawsuits and served as a phenomenal mentor during my time at the Law Office. Arlinda Locklear, a Lumbee tribe citizen, served as outside counsel for the majority of these lawsuits. Among her vast accomplishments in the arena of federal Indian law, she is well known as the first Native American woman to argue a case in front of the United States Supreme Court. As I was leaving the Law Office, the Village's challenges to the continuing existence of the reservation were turning toward litigation. James and Arlinda saw this case through, and their chapter provides their perspectives on that case.

Despite being surrounded by so many people dedicated to fighting for tribal sovereignty, this nonstop litigation was a key factor in my desire to return to school, seek a PhD, find alternative ways to overcome our obstacles, and eventually switch career paths. I obtained my PhD in 2014 and left the Oneida Law Office for a position as an assistant professor at the University of Minnesota Duluth in 2016. My dissertation was a case study of cooperative land use planning on the Oneida reservation. While the issues permeated beyond Nation–Village relationships, those relationships unquestionably informed the study. The findings of my study are reiterated in the conclusion of this book. Their meaning is abundantly clear when one understands the details of the litigious relationship between the Nation and the Village. In the meantime, I think the dedication to my dissertation is wholly appropriate to get this book started. Here it is:

I dedicate this study to my children and those of their generation. They will inherit the legacy we create today, just as we have inherited the legacy of our own forefathers. Throughout my pursuit of higher education and my career as an attorney, I have gained an appreciation for the work our forefathers accomplished in preserving tsi niyukwalihotʌ (our ways) and restoring our land base. They have done so in the wake of generations of federal policy aimed at assimilating Indian people into mainstream society and breaking up tribal landholdings. While we cannot turn back the clock to rewrite history, we can learn to accept reality, adapt, and move forward in a positive manner.

As a result of our history, people from many different backgrounds now share the Oneida reservation, and several different governments administer their laws within this same shared space. This is our reality today. My goals for the future include instilling in my children the values that will help them adapt and move forward in a positive manner. I want them to have pride in being ukwehu·wé (of the original people), of being Onʌyoteʔa·ká (Oneida). I also have faith they can move beyond simple tolerance of those that are different from them. I believe they can accept others with open minds and that others will accept them. I anticipate they will find new ways to work together as a community and refrain from attempts to dominate and oppress their fellow community members. As a community, if we can start demonstrating these values today, this can be the legacy we leave for our children's generation.

CHAPTER 1

The Oneida Nation and the Oneida Indian Reservation in Wisconsin, 1821–1880

JAMES W. OBERLY

KEY TERMS IN THIS CHAPTER

• Treaty

THE EMIGRATION OF THE NEW YORK INDIANS TO WISCONSIN, 1821–1837

In 1821, an emigrating party of Oneidas from New York, along with members of other New York tribal nations, signed a treaty with the Menominee and Winnebago Indians, and the next year with the Menominee Indians alone, to sell or share the lands of the Menominee and Winnebago tribes, amounting to as much as eight million acres of land.[1] The Menominees repudiated any such understanding of the treaties and instead insisted that they had merely consented to allow the New York tribes to live among them as guests.[2] By 1825, the emigrating Oneidas had established a settlement on Duck Creek, upstream from the west shore of Green Bay, and northwest of the small settlement at Green Bay, then a part of the Michigan Territory.[3]

The United States was not a signatory party to the 1821 or 1822 treaties but took note of it in correspondence received by Secretary of War John C. Calhoun and President James Monroe.[4] At the beginning of the new John Quincy Adams administration, the United States called a

15

grand treaty council in the summer of 1825 at Prairie du Chien, inviting all the Great Lakes and Upper Mississippi tribes to discuss the definition of boundaries as a means of peacekeeping.[5] Article 8 of the 1825 treaty attempted to define the Menominee country. The effort proved impossible because the United States acknowledged that the cession by the Menominees to the New York Indians was itself unmapped.

The U.S. representatives and the tribal leaders assembled at Lake Butte des Morts in 1827 to resolve the disputes from the 1821 and 1822 intertribal treaties, but once again, they could not agree on the extent of a land cession for the New York Indians. Although the treaty negotiators failed to win the consent of the Menominees, they did get representatives of that tribe to agree to allow the president of the United States to continue to seek a homeland in Wisconsin for the New York Indians. All parties further agreed on one matter: education mattered, and the United States agreed to spend $1,500 on teachers and schools for the Chippewas (Ojibwes), Menominees, Winnebagos (Ho-Chunks), and New York Indians. The United States agreed to make that payment in perpetuity and did continue to make its annual payments for the next several decades. This 1827 treaty provision was the first time that Congress authorized payments from the U.S. Treasury for the benefit of the relocated New York Indians in present-day Wisconsin.[6]

Secretary of War John Henry Eaton took the lead in the spring of 1830 to resolve the long-running dispute between the New York Indians and the Menominee Indians. The solution that the secretary and President Andrew Jackson had in mind was a land purchase by the United States from the Menominee Indians for the benefit of the New York Indians. Secretary Eaton wrote of his intention to fulfill the 1827 treaty obligation and to provide a permanent homeland "within that claimed and owned by the Menominie [sic] and Winnebago Indians and establish the boundaries of the same for the accommodation of the New York Indians."[7]

Secretary Eaton appointed three men as commissioners to the New York Indians and to the Menominee Indians and gave them explicit instructions as to what he expected the commissioners to accomplish. The secretary did not side with the New York Indians in their claim for eight million acres of land in Wisconsin, but he did want to establish a permanent homeland for them. It was this balance between not disturbing the Menominee and Ho-Chunk occupants of the trans–Green Bay region on one hand and providing sufficient land for the New York Indians on the other that Secretary Eaton urged on his appointed treaty commissioners:

> The Indians in the State of New York number, it is believed, at this time, about 2420; and they claim about 131,640 acres of lands, which is a little over 54 acres to each individual. This view is not given to govern you in limiting the New York Indians to a like quantity at Green Bay—for it would be proper, doubtless, to allow them a quantity fully adequate to all the demands which, as an agricultural people, they ought to possess.[8]

Secretary Eaton gave no instructions to his treaty commissioners to divide up the proposed New York Indian tract of according to any particular formula. There was nothing in his instructions to his treaty commissioners to conduct a survey of the proposed New York Indian tract that would result in individual allotments in severalty. Rather, he expected that the New York Indians would hold their lands in common. He instructed his commissioners of the intention of the United States that "the country the right and title to which will be in the New York Indians and their posterity and upon which they will be protected in the same."[9]

For more than three weeks in August 1830 the treaty commission held councils between the New York Indians and the Menominee Indians. The U.S. treaty commissioners asked Daniel Bread, the Oneida leader of the First Christian Party at Duck Creek, to suggest boundaries for a land cession by the Menominees to benefit the New York Indians. Bread proposed a tract that would have totaled about 850,000 acres. That was more land than the commissioners had in mind. Bread and the treaty commissioners examined different maps of the Wisconsin lands in the Michigan Territory and asked their surveyor, Albert G. Ellis, to draft a cession map.[10]

Later that fall, the president and the secretary of war invited representatives of all the parties to Washington to reach a settlement with the direct intervention of the highest officials in the Executive Branch. The parties moved the negotiations to Washington, D.C., in January 1831, and finally, by February 8, reached an agreement that the United States and the Menominees could sign.[11] The proposed lands reserved to the New York Indians that the secretary of war envisioned expanded to a half million-acre bloc, upon the belief that as many as five thousand New York Indians would move to the Green Bay–region tract. The five-hundred-thousand-acre "New York Indian Tract" as described in the treaty of February 8, 1831, included the Duck Creek settlements of the emigrating Oneidas:

> The country hereby ceded to the United States, for the benefit of the New York Indians, contains by estimation about five hundred thousand acres, and includes all their improvements on the west side of Fox river. As it is intended for a home for the several tribes of the New York Indians, who may be residing upon the lands at the expiration of three years from this date, and for none others, the President of the United States is hereby empowered to apportion the lands among the actual occupants at that time, so as not to assign any tribe a greater number of acres than may be equal to one hundred for each soul actually settled upon the lands. . . . It is distinctly understood that the lands hereby ceded to the United States for the New York Indians, are to be held by those tribes, under such tenure as the Menomonee Indians now hold their lands.[12]

The Jackson administration returned to the subject of homelands for the New York Indians in a subsequent treaty of October 25, 1832. That treaty definitively established three reserved tracts in Wisconsin: one for the New York Indians, understood as the Six Nations; one for the Stockbridge-Munsees; and one for the Brothertown Indians.[13] The treaty cessions that the United States obtained from the Menominees resulted in three sizable reserved tracts: 46,080 acres for the Stockbridge and Munsee tribes on the east shore of Lake Winnebago; 23,040 acres for the Brothertown tribe adjacent to the Stockbridge and Munsee reserve; and 500,000 acres for the New York tribes, to include the Oneida Indians living on Duck Creek.[14] The treaty gave the New York tribes three years to move from their homelands to the tract; after that date, the treaty anticipated that the secretary of war would determine whether, indeed, five thousand New York Indians had relocated to the Michigan Territory. If not, the treaty contemplated a reduction in size of the five-hundred-thousand-acre tract. A map drawn in 1834 by the General Land Office shows the location of the three reserved tracts (see fig. 3).[15] The 1834 map was based on a survey completed by Albert G. Ellis. That survey ran lines that traced the exterior boundaries of the New York Indian Tract, the Stockbridge-Munsee Tract, and the Brothertown Tract. Surveyor Ellis did not attempt to run interior lines within the tracts, either to mark off 640-acre sections within townships and ranges to correspond to the U.S. public domain. Nor did Surveyor Ellis attempt to subdivide the five-hundred-thousand-acre New York Indian Tract into five thousand separate hundred-acre parcels.

The Jackson administration did not wait long to see whether the full complement of five thousand New York Indians had made the move to the Michigan Territory to make permanent the boundaries of the treaty-created New York Indian Tract. Instead, the administration in 1836 sent a treaty commissioner to Duck Creek, in what was by then the new Wisconsin Territory, to negotiate a removal treaty whereby the Oneidas and scattered Tuscaroras and St. Regis Indians in the New York Indian Tract would be removed to lands among the Osage Indians in present-day Kansas. The U.S. Senate rejected that 1836 treaty because of fraudulent activities on the part of the U.S. treaty commissioner.[16]

The United States did not give up, however, on the idea of removing New York Indians to the Osage Country. In the winter of 1837–38, the United States sent a treaty commissioner to New York State to negotiate a move to the trans-Missouri country with the various New York tribes. In the treaty signed on January 15, 1838, the New York tribes agreed to move and to renounce any interest in the five-hundred-thousand-acre New York Indian Tract in the Wisconsin Territory. The first article of the treaty reserved from sale a portion of the New York Indian Tract "on which a part of the New York Indians now reside." The parcel reserved

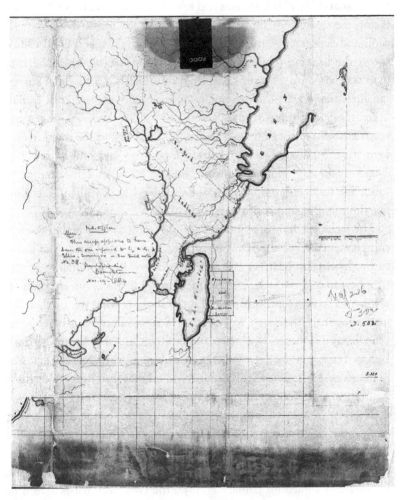

The New York Indian Tract from the 1831 treaty with the Menominees.

under Article 1 included the Duck Creek settlements of the Oneidas, but without specific mention of those settlements. The treaty further stated, "the lands secured to them by patent under this treaty shall never be included in any State or Territory of this Union."[17]

The Treaty of February 3, 1838, and Its Stipulation

Oneida leaders from Duck Creek feared the prospect of a second attempt to remove them from Wisconsin and instead sought permission from the U.S. Indian Agent at Green Bay to negotiate directly with the Van Buren administration in Washington, D.C. Once again, the Oneida people were led by Daniel Bread and by the Episcopalian missionary minister to the Duck Creek Oneidas, the Reverend Solomon Davis. Chief Bread, Rev. Davis, and four other Oneidas from Duck Creek traveled to Washington, D.C., in January 1838 and entered negotiations with the U.S. commissioner of Indian affairs about the future of the New York Indian Tract in Wisconsin. The result was a treaty signed February 3, 1838, between the United States and two parties of emigrating Oneidas on Duck Creek.[18] One group was called the First Christian Party, and a second group was called the Orchard Party. The First Christian Party adhered to the Episcopalian Church, and the Orchard Party to the Methodist Church.[19]

Article One of the February 3, 1838, treaty stated that the First Christian and Orchard parties ceded to the United States all their interest in the New York Indian Tract. This completed the cession that the New York tribes had done of the same tract almost three weeks earlier at Buffalo Creek.[20]

Article Two, however, called upon the United States to reserve from the ceded New York Indian tract a portion for the two Oneida parties:

> From the foregoing cession there shall be reserved to the said Indians to be held as other Indian lands are held a tract of land containing one hundred (100) acres, for each individual, and the lines of which shall be so run as to include all their settlements and improvements in the vicinity of Green Bay.

The element of continuity stands out in this treaty article. The size of the reserved tract was based on the same formula of one hundred acres per capita. The Oneida reservation had the same land tenure status as the New York Indian Tract in that the lands were to be held in common, that is, "as other Indian lands are held." The treaty also called upon the United States to pay the First Christian Party $30,500 and the Orchard Party $3,000 for undefined services rendered to the United States in obtaining the New York Indian Tract. In effect, the United States was paying the two Oneida parties a combined sum of $33,500, or about seven cents an acre, for ceding what turned out to be about 435,000 acres of the New York Indian Tract. The treaty provided that the First Christian Party and the Orchard Party would hold the lands together as the "said parties of Oneida Indians." There was nothing in the treaty text or in any of the documents in the Indian Office file about the treaty concerning the division of the reserved lands between the First Christian Party and the Orchard Party.

On April 24, 1838, the U.S. Senate took up the matter of giving its advice and consent to the February 3, 1838, treaty. On May 12, 1838, in a Saturday session, the Senate debated and approved the February 3, 1838, treaty unanimously, thirty-three in favor and none opposed.[21] Despite U.S. Senate approval in May 1838, the Treaty of February 3, 1838, was not self-implementing. The United States had to perform three interconnected actions before the treaty could be put into effect. First, the United States had to take a census of the Nation; second, the United States had to conduct a survey setting aside a quantity of land that was one hundred times in acreage the population figure tallied in the tribal census; third, Congress, beginning with the House of Representatives, had to appropriate money to implement the provisions of the treaty. These actions eventually took place, but not in the order listed here. Instead, the first action was appropriation by Congress of money to implement the treaty. The House and Senate included $37,074 for implementing the terms of the treaty. The appropriations bill to fund the activities of the Indian Office passed Congress and became law with President Martin Van Buren's signature on July 7, 1838. That appropriation gave the secretary of war and his commissioner of Indian affairs the authority to implement the provisions of the treaty of February 3, 1838, including the payment of claims and the delineation of the reserved lands.[22]

The commissioner of Indian affairs waited another month after congressional appropriation of the money to begin the U.S. part of the first two steps of the implementation. The commissioner then gave Henry Dodge, the territorial governor, the task of finding a treaty commissioner to do the work of stipulation. The governor finally succeeded in November 1838, when he secured the services of a treaty commissioner, Henry S. Baird of Green Bay, and a surveyor, John Suydam, also of Green Bay.[23] The appointment came just in time for the commissioner to include news of it in his annual report, dated November 25, 1838.[24] Once appointed, Baird and Suydam did their work quickly. Baird counted 654 Oneida Indians among the Duck Creek settlements, and Suydam laid out the external boundaries of the reservation containing 65,400 acres in size. The reservation was rectangular in shape, roughly twelve miles by eighty miles in size, but with careful attention paid to existing land claims on the eastern border, giving the tract a saw-toothed shape on one edge.[25] Baird wrote to the commissioner of Indian affairs on December 15, 1838, that he and his surveyor had finished their work: "The survey of the land is completed, the examination of the claims closed, and the result declared to the Indians; all to their perfect satisfaction."[26] Surveyor Suydam prepared a map and field notes showing the exterior boundaries of the reservation (see fig. 4), and, along with Baird's report of his claims settling under Article 3, these documents were sent to the territorial governor, Henry Dodge, in Madison, and then on to the commissioner of Indian affairs in Washington.[27]

In 1839, when first Governor Dodge and then federal officials at the War Department saw the results of Baird and Suydam's work, they declared the Treaty of February 3, 1838, implemented.[28] The commissioner of the General Land Office (GLO) notified the commissioner of Indian affairs that there would be a delay in surveying the ceded portion of the New York Indian Tract because of questions related to a land cession by the Menominee Indians under a separate treaty of 1836.[29] Not until 1844 did the GLO complete the survey of the 434,600 acres

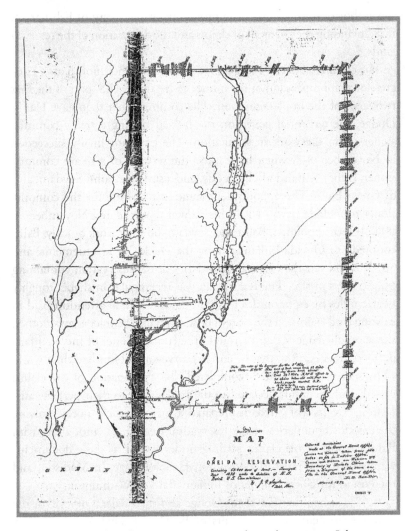

Map of the Oneida Indian Reservation, 1838, drawn by surveyor John Suydam. The February 3, 1838, treaty between the United States and the Oneida Nation stipulated that the survey of the Oneida Indian Reservation shall "include all their settlements and improvements in the vicinity of Green Bay." Suydam's map shows that as of 1838 the Oneidas had built a thriving community of houses, churches, sawmills, and grist mills along a twelve-mile stretch of Duck Creek.

ceded under the January 15 and February 3, 1838, treaties. That 1844 survey, conducted by Albert G. Ellis, located the blaze marks and surveyor posts that Suydam had left in 1838 as he ran the exterior lines of the lands reserved for the First Christian and Orchard parties.[30]

Finally, in May 1845, President Polk announced that the lands in the ceded portion of the New York Indian Tract would be put up for public auction at the Green Bay Land Office. Specifically, on May 9, the president issued a public proclamation that explicitly recognized the Oneida Indian reservation and, furthermore, recognized that the reservation was not part of the public domain and therefore, not available for non-Indians to enter land claims. No non-Indian would-be settler could buy land within the reservation; no such settler could make a preemption or "squatter" claim on the reservation. The United States kept the Oneida Indian reservation for the exclusive use of the Oneida Indians. President James Knox Polk took care to instruct employees in the General Land Office about which tracts of public lands were available and made it clear that the Oneida reservation was off limits.[31]

The Treaty of February 3, 1838, stated that the lands were "to be held as other Indian lands are held," a phrase that also appeared in the February 8, 1831, Menominee treaty and numerous other treaties the United States negotiated and the Senate ratified during the Jacksonian Era. This was not an idyllic "as long as the waters run" or "as long as the grass is green" statement about a permanent tribal homeland, but neither was there any limit placed on the length of time that the Nation could stay on its reservation.

Until the 1980s, no student of the Treaty of February 3, 1838, sought to interpret the treaty as having created 654 separate trust parcels of one hundred acres apiece. The anthropologist James Clifton offered such a radically different interpretation of the treaty language when he prepared a research report for Brown and Outagamie Counties in the early 1980s when both local governments had a dispute with the Nation. Clifton based his novel interpretation of the treaty upon the difference between the language of Article II and that of Article III: the former referred to a "tract" reserved to the use of the Oneidas, but the latter referred to "tracts" in the plural. Clifton deduced that the reference to "tracts" meant that the United States never set aside a reservation in 1838 for the benefit of the Nation from the old New York Indian Tract. Instead, said Clifton, the Nation requested, and the United States obliged, the setting up of allotments for every member of the Nation.[32]

Clifton's interpretation was not followed by Brown and Outagamie Counties in the 1980s, nor by the State of Wisconsin when it initiated litigation in the mid-1990s over the exact boundary lines of the Oneida reservation. However, more than three decades after Clifton devised his interpretation of the February 3, 1838, treaty, the Village of Hobart adopted his views in litigation asking a federal court to declare that the Oneida reservation never existed. The Village cast its Clifton-inspired argument as a matter of the "plain language" of the treaty, that is, "tracts" in the plural could mean only 654 separate 100-acre reservations with no role for the Nation in exercising sovereign powers over the whole 65,400 acres.

As additional evidence for its position, the Village pointed to an abortive set of treaty negotiations in 1838 and 1839 between the U.S. representative who negotiated the Buffalo Creek treaty—former congressman Ransom Gillet—on the one hand and some Oneidas who had not represented the Nation at the February 3, 1838, treaty negotiations on the other side. The dissident Oneida wrote to President Van Buren in October 1838 indicating their unhappiness with Daniel Bread's leadership and with the way that annuities were distributed under the February 3, 1838, treaty. They stated that they would be open to removal from the Oneida reservation if they could exchange reservation lands at the Duck Creek settlement in the Wisconsin Territory for lands west of the Mississippi River "out of the reach of the White Settlements." The letter was signed or witnessed by as many as 190 members of the Nation.[33]

President Van Buren passed the letter on to Commissioner of Indian Affairs T. Hartley Crawford, and in turn the commissioner in December 1838 appointed Gillet to proceed under the authority Congress had granted the president under the Indian Removal Act of 1830. The goal, as it was in 1836, was to negotiate yet another removal treaty by which the Oneida Nation would be removed west of the Mississippi River.[34] The draft treaty that Gillet sent to the commissioner of Indian affairs called for individual Oneidas to exchange their right to 100 acres of land on the Oneida reservation for a future 320 acres somewhere in the trans-Mississippi and trans-Missouri country that was the homeland of the Osage Indians. Commissioner Gillet wrote that he dealt with four Oneida representatives, who claimed that they represented unstated others. However, only two of the dissident Oneida journeyed to Buffalo, New York, to meet with Gillet, and when Commissioner Crawford learned this fact, he declined to present the treaty to the president for his approval and to the U.S. Senate for ratification.[35]

The draft treaty that Gillet presented to Crawford never specified any particular one-hundred-acre parcels that would be relinquished, nor did it describe what would become of the Oneida reservation and the members of the Nation if some members refused to participate and instead chose to remain in Wisconsin. At the same time that Gillet was negotiating a removal treaty with the dissident Oneidas, Commissioner Baird and Surveyor Suydam were at work in Wisconsin completing the survey of the Oneida reservation. Suydam's map, shown as Figure 4, is the best evidence that the U.S. commissioners tasked with seeing the February 3, 1838, treaty to "stipulation" (completion) understood that the treaty created one reservation of 65,400 acres for the Nation, not 654 separate ones.

The abortive negotiations that Gillet conducted are best understood today as yet another attempt to remove the Oneida Indians from their homeland in Wisconsin, and not as some sort of contemporary understanding about the terms of the February 3, 1838, treaty. Even into the late 1840s, the U.S. Indian agent would raise the matter of the Oneidas signing a removal treaty and moving to the Great Plains, but, as the agent noted in 1847, "The Oneidas are not disposed to sell or move."[36] Also, neither was there any contemplation that the president or other federal officials could alter the land-holding tenure, as, for example, was the case in subsequent treaties in the 1850s that called for reserved lands to be allotted in severalty.[37]

THE RESERVATION IN THE
LUMBERING ERA, 1867–1880

In the years after the Civil War, Wisconsin lumbermen sought to acquire direct access to pine timber on the Oneida, Menominee, and
Stockbridge-Munsee Indian reservations. They wanted to bypass the
existing arrangements whereby tribal members at the three reservations
cut, banked, rafted, and sometimes milled their own timber. The leader
of what was soon called the "Timber Ring" was the Republican Party
leader and congressman from Oshkosh, Philetus Sawyer. Working with
Morgan L. Martin, the U.S. Indian agent at Green Bay, Congressman
Sawyer convinced the commissioner of Indian affairs and the secretary
of the interior in March 1868 to order the halt of all timber cutting and
sales on all three reservations. In the case of the Oneida reservation, the
reason was that individual Oneidas cutting tribal timber were taking
from the "common property." In June 1868, the U.S. Senate requested a
report from the secretary of the interior and particularly wished to know
the following of the secretary:

> whether he has issued any order, or adopted any regulation, prohibiting
> the individuals of the Oneida tribe of Indians from cutting and remov-
> ing timber from the common lands of the tribe; and, if so, under what
> laws such prohibition is sanctioned, and what penalties are imposed for a
> violation of such rule.[38]

The secretary and his commissioner of Indian affairs explained their
reasoning in a July 1868 reply to the Senate: "Individual Indians have
not the right, and cannot be permitted to cut and dispose of the common property of the Tribe for their individual uses and purposes."[39]

The issue of logging on reservations did not end with the secretary's
order to Agent Martin in the spring of 1868. Tribal governments continued to issue permits to tribal members to engage in on-reservation
logging. The issue divided the tribal body politic at Oneida into two
groups, one in favor of logging on tribal lands, in defiance of the Andrew
Johnson administration, and an opposing group that favored allotment

in severalty so that individual Oneida Indians could log their own individually owned parcels. An 1868 petition by the opposition group called for the United States to reinterpret the February 3, 1838, treaty as an allotment promise and called upon the president and the Interior Department to give each Oneida Indian a one-hundred-acre parcel or, because of population growth, fewer than one hundred acres per person.[40]

The 1868 petition of the Oneida chiefs raised the idea that the February 3, 1838, treaty could be interpreted as an allotment-in-severalty promise. However, no U.S. government authority then or subsequently accepted this view of the treaty's intent. This includes the Congress, the federal courts, the Office of Indian Affairs, the Interior Department, and the president of the United States. The interpretation about the intent of the February 3, 1838, treaty was not raised again for another 116 years after the 1868 Oneida chiefs' petition, that is, not until the early 1980s, when the county boards of Outagamie and Brown consulted James Clifton, who proposed the interpretation that the true intent of the February 3, 1838, treaty had been to create 654 individual parcels of one hundred acres each for 654 individual Oneida Indians.

The federal courts became involved in the Oneida Nation's affairs during the years 1869–74, as a result of the actions taken by U.S. Indian Agent Morgan L. Martin and his superiors in the Interior Department in their attempts to stop tribal members from logging on the reservation. In 1869, the OIA and the Interior Department pressed the U.S. attorney for the Eastern District of Wisconsin to commence criminal charges against lumbermen for on-reservation logging. The resulting case in 1869 was filed against George Cook, a lumberman who operated a sawmill just outside the boundaries of the Oneida reservation. The U.S. attorney decided to charge Cook with the unlikely offense of denying timber to the United States Navy. The U.S. commissioner in Milwaukee, Francis Bloodgood, who sat as a trial judge for the Eastern District, dismissed the criminal charges against Cook for purchasing logs cut by tribal members. Commissioner Bloodgood wrote:

> By the treaty of Feby 3 1838 between the U.S. and the First Christian and Orchard parties of the Oneida Indians . . . it was provided *that this*

reservation to the said Indians should be held as other Indian lands are held.
I can find no other regulations by the Government of the U.S. by treaty or
legislation changing or effecting the tenure [emphasis in the original] by
which these tribes of the Oneidas were to hold, and enjoy this reservation
thus acquired.[41]

Commissioner Bloodgood's opinion shows that he read the 1831 and
1838 treaties closely. His opinion further shows that he did not accept
the idea that the February 8, 1838, treaty was in any sense an allotment
treaty. To the contrary, his opinion held the view that the Oneidas were
to enjoy their lands in common, not merely in the same way as other
Indian lands, but precisely in the same way the Menominee Indians
had enjoyed the same lands up until ceding them to the US in 1831. In
short, the Oneida Indians had every right to cut timber on their own
reservation and sell the logs to non-Indian lumbermen.

The change in partisan leadership of the Office of Indian Affairs
(OIA) and the Interior Department from the Johnson to the Ulysses S.
Grant administrations did not change the determination of the executive branch to use the federal courts to dissuade Oneida tribal members
from timber cutting on their reservations and non-Indian lumbermen
from buying the logs. In the spring of 1870, the U.S. attorney, at the
urging of the commissioner of Indian affairs and the secretary of the
interior, began a new set of civil suits against lumbermen and some
tribal members in the trial court for the Eastern District of Wisconsin.
The same unfortunate George Cook was again summoned to court, this
time not on a criminal charge of denying timber to the U.S. Navy (the
1869 charge) but rather for civil "replevin" (seizure) of U.S. property.
Along with Cook, Nathaniel C. Foster of Green Bay was charged with
replevin of federal property in purchasing sawlogs from Oneida Nation
timber cutters. The U.S. Attorney filed seven suits in February 1870 and
another half-dozen in April, many of them against the same defendants.
Petit juries were not impressed with the government's case, in one instance finding a verdict for the United States and ordering a judgment
of six cents in damages.[42] Although the criminal prosecutions and the
civil proceedings failed in federal district court, eventually the United

States prevailed in an 1874 U.S. Supreme Court decision in the case of *U.S. v. Cook*, the same beleaguered George Cook who had been defending himself in the Eastern District since 1869. Writing for the Court, the chief justice said:

> The right of the Indians in the land from which the logs were taken was that of occupancy alone. They had no power of alienation except to the United States. The fee was in the United States, subject only to this right of occupancy. This is the title by which other Indians hold their lands. It was so decided by this court as early as 1823, in *Johnson v. McIntosh*. The authority of that case has never been doubted. The right of the Indians to their occupancy is as sacred as that of the United States to the fee, but it is only a right of occupancy.[43]

The chief justice did not address the February 3, 1838, treaty in his opinion. However, the head notes prepared by the clerk of the Court in 1874 indicate awareness of the 1831 treaty with the Menominees and of the February 3, 1838, treaty with the Oneidas. Moreover, the clerk's headnotes quote from both treaties, and specifically from the 1838 one that the reserved tract of about sixty-five-thousand acres was "to be held as other Indian lands are held."[44]

CONCLUSION

The basis for Oneida Nation territorial jurisdiction in present-day Wisconsin is the set of treaties negotiated and signed in the first half of the nineteenth century, starting with the intertribal treaties of 1821 and 1822 and then continuing to the U.S. treaties with the Menominee Indians (1832) and the U.S. treaties with the New York Indians (January 1838) and the Oneida Indians (February 1838). Decades of disputes came to an end when President Polk proclaimed the opening of certain land districts in the Territory of Wisconsin in 1845 and at the same time announced that the lands of the Oneida Indian reservation were for the exclusive use of the people of the Oneida Nation, to be held in common. During the 1830s and into the 1840s, the Oneida Nation resisted any further removals and made a homeland of the Oneida Indian reservation. Over these same years, the political economy of the Green Bay and Fox River Valley region changed from fur trapping to pine lumbering. The demand for pine by Green Bay–area sawmills led to a crisis on the Oneida Indian reservation over the question of ownership of trees. The Oneida Nation, in cooperation with the U.S. Indian agent, had controlled access to logging on the reservation, but political changes in Washington, backed up by a U.S. Supreme Court decision, took away the Nation's control over the licensing of the sale of its own timber. As the population and economy grew in the counties surrounding the reservation, Brown and Outagamie, pressure grew to turn to allotment in severalty as the way for Oneida Indians and non-Native settlers alike to exploit more fully the resources of the reservation.

NOTES

1. Treaty between the Menomini, Winnebago, and New York Indians, 1821, and Treaty between the Menomini and New York Indians, 1822, in *Documents Relating to the Negotiation of Ratified and Unratified Treaties with Various Tribes of Indians, 1801–69*, Records of the Bureau of Indian Affairs, Record Group 75, NAM T-494, Reel 1.

2. James W. Oberly, "Decision on Duck Creek: Two Green Bay Reservations and Their Boundaries, 1816–1996," *American Indian Culture and Research Journal* 24, no. 3 (2000): 39–76.

3. Albert G. Ellis, "Some Account of the Advent of the New York Indians into Wisconsin," in *Wisconsin Historical Collections* (Madison: State Printer, 1857), 415–49; Ebenezer Childs, "Recollections of Wisconsin since 1820," in *Wisconsin Historical Collections*, vol. 4, (Madison: State Printer, 1859) 153–95; Henry S. Baird, "Early History of Northern Wisconsin," in *Wisconsin Historical Collections*, vol. 4, (Madison: State Printer, 1859) 197–221.

4. Ellis, "Advent of the New York Indians in Wisconsin," 428.

5. "An Act to Enable the President to Hold Treaties with Certain Indian Tribes, and for Other Purposes," Act of May 25, 1824, 4, *Statutes at Large*, 35–36. See also Ronald N. Satz, *Chippewa Treaty Rights: The Reserved Rights of Wisconsin's Chippewa Indians* (Madison: University of Wisconsin Press, 1994).

6. "Treaty with the Chippewa, etc., August 11, 1827," 281–83.

7. John Henry Eaton to treaty commissioners, June 15, 1830, in "Letters Received from the Green Bay Agency," Records of the Bureau of Indian Affairs, Record Group 75, NAM M-234, Roll 315.

8. Eaton to treaty commissioners, June 15, 1830.

9. Eaton to treaty commissioners, June 15, 1830.

10. "Journal of Proceedings of a Treaty with the Menominee Indians," August 25, 1830, in "Letters Received from the Green Bay Agency," Records of the Bureau of Indian Affairs, Record Group 75 (hereafter RG-75, LR), NAM-234, Roll 315.

11. "Treaty with the Menominee, February 8, 1831," Charles J. Kappler, *Indian Affairs: Laws and Treaties*, vol. 2 (Washington, DC: Government Printing Office, 1902), 319.

12. "Treaty with the Menominee, February 8, 1831," Kappler, *Indian Affairs*, II, 320.

13. Treaty with the Menominee, October 25, 1832," Kappler, *Indian Affairs*, 377.

14. Charles C. Royce, *Schedule of Indian Land Cessions*, in *House Document* No. 736, 56th Congress, 1st Session (1898), 731–32, 742–45.

15. General Land Office, "Map of New York Indian Tract" (1834). See John Carter Bloom, ed., *Territorial Papers of the United States: Microfilm Edition*, NAM M-236, Roll 122, Map 78.

16. Laurence Hauptman, Conspiracy of Interests: Iroquois Dispossession and the Rise of New York State (Syracuse: Syracuse University Press, 2001).

17. "Treaty with the New York Indians, January 15, 1838," in Kappler, *Indian Affairs*, II, 502–16.

18. "Treaty with the Oneida, February 3, 1838," in Kappler, *Indian Affairs*, II, 517–18. The manuscript of the treaty is reproduced in "Ratified Indian Treaties," Records of the Bureau of Indian Affairs, Record Group 75, NAM M-668, Roll 6, Treaty 232.

19. Colonel Boyd to Commissioner of Indian Affairs, June 15, 1838, in "Letters Received from the Green Bay Agency," Roll 317.

20. Treaty of February 3, 1838.

21. *Senate Executive Journal*, 25th Congress, 2nd Session (1838), 110.

22. "An Act Making Appropriations for the Current and Contingent Expenses of the Indian Department," 25th Congress, Second Session (July 7, 1838), *Statutes at Large of the United States*, vol. 5 (Boston: Little, Brown, 1856), 300.

23. Governor Henry Dodge to Henry S. Baird, November 21, 1838, RG-75, LR.

24. Annual Report of the Commissioner of Indian Affairs, November 25, 1838, 504, 561 (hereafter cited as ARCIA).

25. Oberly, "Decision on Duck Creek: Two Green Bay Reservations, 1816–1996"; "Census of Oneida Indians," December 12, 1838; "Field Notes and Plat of Oneida Indian Reservation," December 12, 1838. Both the 1838 census and the 1838 surveyor notes are in "Letters Received from the Green Bay Agency," Records of the Bureau of Indian Affairs, Record Group 75 (hereafter RG-75, LR, NAM-234, Roll 315.

26. Henry S. Baird to Commissioner of Indian Affairs, December 15, 1838, RG-75, LR, NAM M234, Reel 317.

27. Henry S. Baird to Territorial Governor Dodge, RG-75, LR, December 19, 1838, LR, NAM M234, Reel 317.

28. Governor Henry Dodge to Commissioner of Indian Affairs, January 2, 1839, RG-75, LR, Reel 317.

29. Commissioner of the General Land Office to Commissioner of Indian Affairs, February 19, 1839, RG-75, LR, Reel 318.

30. "Received with Surveyor General's Letter of 12 April 1844." *Territorial Papers of the United States: Territory of Wisconsin, 1836–1848. A Microfilm Supplement.* NAM-236, Roll 122, Entry 97.

31. Presidential Proclamation of May 9, 1845. *Territorial Papers of the United States: Territory of Wisconsin, 1836–1848. A Microfilm Supplement.* NAM-236, Roll 122, Entry 393.

32. "Oneida Tribe," Box 14, Folder 67, James Clifton Papers, Clarke Historical Library, Central Michigan University.

33. "Petition to the President by Oneida Indians," *Territorial Papers of the United States: Wisconsin Territory* (Washington, D.C.: Government Printing Office, 1969), Vol. 27, 1078–87.

34. T. Hartley Crawford to Ransom H. Gillet, December 4, 1838, Records of the Bureau of Indian Affairs: Letters Received, 1824–1881, Record Group 75, National Archives Microfilm M-234, Reel, 317, frames 440–41.

35. T. Hartley Crawford to Joel Poinsett, March 21, 1839, Records of the Bureau of Indian Affairs: Letters Received, 1824–1881, Record Group 75, National Archives Microfilm M-234, Reel, 317, frames 713–15.

36. ARCIA, 1847, 97.

37. For example, "Treaty with the Stockbridge and Munsee, February 5, 1856," in Kappler, *Indian Affairs*, II, 744.

38. "Letter of Secretary of the Interior," Senate Executive Documents, No. 72, 40th Congress, 2nd Session (1868).

39. "Letter of Secretary of the Interior."

40. "Petition of Oneida Chiefs" to president and Congress, November 18, 1868, in RG-75, LR, Roll 326, frames 300–309.

41. Opinion of U.S. Commissioner Francis Bloodgood, United States v. Cook, Eastern District of Wisconsin (February 27, 1869) in RG-75, LR, Roll 326, frames 27–42.

42. Docket, United States v. Foster, Eastern District of Wisconsin (1870).

43. United States v. Cook, 86 U.S. Reports, 591 (1874).

44. United States v. Cook, 86 U.S. Reports, 591 (1874).

CHAPTER 2

From Allotment to the Indian New Deal, 1887–1934

FREDERICK E. HOXIE

KEY TERMS IN THIS CHAPTER

- Allotment
- Fee patents

In the decade prior to the passage of the General Allotment Act in early 1887, the battle lines established in disputes both within the tribe and with local white businessmen during the previous two decades remained fixed. Non-Indians repeatedly urged the division of the reservation into individual homesteads, while tribal members resisted. Policymakers in Washington were also divided, but by 1887 they reached a consensus that all reservations should ultimately be allotted and all Indians "assimilated" into the American mainstream. High-minded reformers backed these ideas as humanitarians, but in Green Bay, merchants and real estate developers welcomed them for another reason: they were good for business.

ONEIDAS VOTE AGAINST ALLOTMENT

The Oneidas were clear: they preferred the status quo. In the spring of 1884, the tribe's agent, D. P. Andrews, reported to the Indian Office that the council had met to respond to the commissioner's inquiry regarding their attitude toward allotment. A clear majority voted "to let the matter remain as is"—that is, to maintain their preserve.[1] When Congress acted in February 1887, it considered a variety of approaches and approved a compromise plan for when and how to begin the allotment process. Under the terms of the Dawes Act, the Chief Executive was authorized, "whenever in his opinion any reservation . . . is advantageous for agricultural and grazing purposes," to direct allotting agents to begin dividing that reserve without first obtaining tribal consent. The law also noted that a tribe's "surplus land"—acreage not needed for allotment—would be opened to non-Indians only after a tribe had agreed to sell it to the United States.[2]

In January 1887, as the debate in Washington over allotment was reaching its conclusion, a group of "sachems and councilors" at Oneida (which included George Doxtator, the leader of the tribe's pro-allotment faction) submitted a petition to the secretary of interior that declared "the bill . . . just meets our wants as a nation." The petitioners declared their support for allotment. But this group went on to note that its members were particularly supportive of Section 11 of the proposed legislation. According to these pro-allotment Oneidas, Section 11 "reads thus: that nothing in this act shall be considered as authorizing the Secretary of the Interior to abolish any reservation until the consent of a majority of the male members twenty-one years of age shall be first had and obtained." Citing this provision of the proposed law, the petitioners added that they "would most earnestly ask your Hon[or] to grant us allowance in this particular matter." Some would accept the law, they noted, while others would not. "In this way, they wrote, we shall not injure any one's feelings, as we wish to do our business harmoniously."[3] Unfortunately for the petitioners, their endorsement was based on an earlier version of the allotment bill. The final statute did not include the Section 11 language they quoted in their appeal.

The confusion over the content of the Dawes Act explains why William Parsons, the government agent assigned to discuss allotment with the tribe, reported his "surprise" when confronted with "the majority . . . [who] had never signified their desire to take their land in severalty." The opposition, he noted, was "very bitter" and "ably led." The special agent insisted, however, that "after considerable difficulty," he "succeeded in getting the tribe to accept allotment." He claimed that two-thirds of the group's members had voted in favor of allotment.[4]

Parsons indicated he would be leaving Green Bay on August 25, so it was unlikely that he witnessed a second tribal gathering on the last day of the month, at which Cornelius Hill and other tribal leaders framed yet another petition to Washington. This remarkable document (endorsed by the Episcopal missionary Edward Goodnough, a longtime opponent of allotment) renewed the tribe's objections to the wholesale division of its lands. Hill and his colleagues conceded that "some parties here" had asked for allotment in the past, because those pro-allotment Oneidas had assumed the division of their estate would be voluntary; the petitioners reported that the community had been surprised when Parsons "told us that the land would be allotted whether we were willing or not." Such an eventuality had never before been considered. Hill and the petitioners added that many of those who voted at the August council to approve allotment "have now determined not to take allotments." The petition noted that the Dawes Act was "a very good law for those to whom it is adapted," but for the Oneidas, "it will be disastrous."[5]

For the next eighteen months, tribal leaders, Indian Office officials, and local politicians debated the application of the Dawes Act to the Oneida reservation. The tribe remained divided. In May 1888, a petition carrying the signatures of Cornelius Hill and missionary Goodnough (and bolstered by 138 additional signatures from Oneida men) repeated this theme. The petitioners asked "our great father" to protect them "against encroachments . . . of our neighbors in Brown and Outagamie Counties." They claimed local non-Indians had "entered into a regular conspiracy with each other and with some of discontented members of the tribe to have our land allotted in severalty." Hill and his colleagues accused their "neighbors" of bribing tribal members and working to undermine the tribal leadership.[6]

The inspiration for this May 1888 petition was a special bill introduced in February by Congressman Thomas R. Hudd (formerly an attorney in Green Bay) that would have ordered the immediate allotment of the reservation and the extension of U.S. citizenship to its residents.[7] In addition to mandating that Oneida allotment would take place at once,

Hudd's bill also shortened the period during which Indians would be prohibited from selling their land from twenty-five years (as provided in the Dawes Act) to five. The congressman declared that "The Oneidas ceased to be Indians, save in name, more than a quarter century ago." Hudd pressed his case, even arguing in a May report to Congress that the residents of the reservation "have declared unanimously for the privilege of citizenship and that they may hold their lands in severalty."[8]

Compromise on the Horizon

By the fall of 1888, the Oneida leadership realized they had no option but to compromise with the powerful forces arrayed against them. A new group of petitioners (which included Cornelius Hill and his former adversary George Doxtator) signed a statement requesting the application of the Dawes Severalty Act to their reservation. They argued that the reservation was suffering from lawlessness because tribal officials had no police authority. (The Indian Office had never responded to their request for support for tribal officials.) As a consequence, they complained that the tribe had "no laws," and tribal members could not apply to local American courts for protection. The petitioners argued that they wished to enjoy the "rights, privileges and immunities of citizenship as it is provided in the Dawes Severalty Bill." They also wanted to block Congressman Hudd. They concluded by reporting that their request rested on "a unanimous vote of the approval of the Dawes bill by the standing officers of this nation." They hoped that this "remedy . . . will settle our difficulties."[9]

The tribe's new unity continued into 1889. During the final days of the postelection congressional session, Hudd's bill won passage in the House. Despite pleas from Green Bay leaders to the tribe to support Hudd's bill, the Oneidas remained opposed and continued to request allotment under the more protective provisions of the Dawes Act. Their determination carried the day. In May, President Benjamin Harrison ordered the Oneida reserve allotted under the provisions of the Dawes Act and appointed Dana Lamb the tribe's special allotting agent.

During the allotment era, the federal government retreated from its long commitment to the protection of American Indian communities.

It ceased to negotiate new treaties with tribes in 1871. The Indian Office created a centrally administered system of Indian schools, and it urged its employees to eradicate traditional Native religious beliefs and to outlaw tribal cultural practices. At the same time, government officials decided to scale back the legal and political rights associated with the U.S. citizenship that had originally been granted all Dawes Act allottees.[10] Federal officials undermined tribal leaders and argued with growing unanimity that Indian communities would have no permanent place in American society.[11]

Allotment across Indian Country

As a consequence of these views, dozens of reservations across the country were completely allotted and their members left with few federal services to assist them. At the Isabella Reserve, in central Michigan, for example, allotment was followed by waves of fraudulent timber and property purchases that drove many of the Saginaw Chippewa people living there into homelessness and poverty. A similar pattern was evident at other Ojibwe reserves in Wisconsin and Minnesota. In the West, the Nez Perce tribe saw its entire reservation allotted and (following the sale of the community's so-called surplus lands) invaded by non-Indian ranchers and farmers. Similar stories unfolded in Washington State, New Mexico, and the Dakotas. Indian Territory, set aside originally for tribes resettled there from other parts of the nation, was completely allotted.[12]

Significantly, however, none of these communities equated allotment with the termination of federal protection. The allotment era produced dramatic changes in Native land tenure, but, instead of gradually disappearing as white people hoped, tribal groups resisted efforts to remake them in the image of non-Indians. And they persisted. The history of their survival is both complex and confusing. On one hand, Native leaders understood the limits of their power. Outnumbered and routinely ignored in the public arena, they could not shape legislation or Indian Office policies. Direct resistance, therefore, was usually doomed. On the other hand, a tribe's efforts to accommodate the demands of outsiders were interpreted frequently as concessions to "civilization" and were therefore often accompanied by community dissent and disagreement.

For these reasons, Native resistance was most effective—as it was among the Oneida—when it was flexible and focused on local issues and strategies to avoid the harshest aspects of government paternalism.[13]

ALLOTMENT SURVEYS OF THE ONEIDA RESERVATION

Special Agent Dana Lamb spent the summer of 1889 determining how many tribal members would be eligible for allotments. By September he reported to the Indian Office that he had identified 1,728 Oneidas who should receive a portion of the 65,244 acre tribal homeland. Because the reserve was not large enough to distribute 160-acre allotments to each family head as the Dawes Act stipulated, the Indian Office ordered Agent Lamb to assign each head of family 90 acres and each single person age 18 or more, 46 acres. Single people under age 18 would receive ten acres.[14] Lamb and his assistant, Charles Kelsey, continued their work through 1890 and submitted a roster of allotments to the Indian Office for approval early in 1891. This approval was granted on September 25, 1891; the Interior Department distributed 1,503 trust patents to tribal members on June 13, 1892. As was the case for all Dawes Act allotments, these trust titles—which barred local governments from imposing property taxes and sale—were intended to remain in effect for twenty-five years—until the summer of 1917. These trust patents also stipulated that the Oneida allottees were now U.S. citizens.

With the arrival of Agents Lamb and Kelsey, allotment became a visible reality on the Oneida reservation. Not surprisingly, despite the fact that Cornelius Hill and other elected tribal leaders had eventually supported the division of tribal lands, a new group in the tribe denounced the process. The *Washington Post* reported in January 1890 that "a delegation of Oneida Indians" had arrived in the capital "asking for a suspension of the work of allotting land to the members of their tribe." The group announced that "the full-bloods of the tribe are a unit in opposition to receiving allotments, and that the half-breeds are the only ones on the reservation who favor it."[15] The members of this anti-allotment delegation were not identified, but a Census Bureau profile of the tribe based on the 1890 national enumeration described this new tribal faction in some detail. The Census Bureau reported the group of anti-allotment activists "styles itself the Indian party. It numbers only about 40 families. . . . The members of this party do not acknowledge any allegiance to the other two parties, respecting no other authority other than that of the United States government. They protest against the allotment of land." The report continued, "A treaty was made years ago, they maintain, in which the government conceded that after their removal to Wisconsin they should remain undisturbed."[16]

While allotment itself had become a fait accompli by 1892, the "Indian Party" activists rejected the process and remained outspoken defenders of Oneida treaty rights and land ownership. A note in the Quaker-sponsored *Friends' Intelligencer* in late 1895 indicated that the "chiefs and head men" at the Oneida agency had charged that white men with farms adjoining the reservation had "stolen four miles of their lands" by manipulating boundary markers in the area.[17] An investigation carried out the following year revealed that the encroachment had occurred on the allotment of Paul Doxtator, a Civil War veteran. When the white landowners rejected the charges against them, the commissioner of Indian affairs (after considerable delay) recommended that the Justice Department take action to protect Doxtator's allotment.[18]

Post-Allotment Fee Patents

Despite the Wisconsin Oneidas' frustrations with Washington and their fears regarding the integrity of the reservation, the 1890s were a relatively calm and prosperous time for them. Their lands were divided into individual homesteads, but the allotment process had little impact on living or subsistence patterns. Restrictions on land sales and leases were firmly in place. Farmers continued to farm, and those engaged in wage labor continued to find work with both their Indian and non-Indian neighbors and in surrounding towns. There is no evidence that individual families fenced off their allotments or that extended kin groups broke up to form individual homesteads operated by nuclear families. Because of restrictions imposed by trust patents, few allotments were sold or leased to outsiders. The Indian Office continued its supervision of the community by designating the head of the tribal school to be tribal "sub-agent" and overseeing the Oneida's tribal police force. As the agent reported in the fall of 1895, the members of the tribe "are apparently happy with their lot."[19]

In the first years of the new century, federal authorities appeared ready to continue in their role as protectors of the tribal estate. In 1901, for example, the acting Indian commissioner assured his superiors in the Interior Department that "there has been no attempt made to obtain legislation authorizing the sale of the allotted lands of the Oneida Indians before the expiration of the [twenty-five-year] trust period. Should any such legislation be proposed," the acting commissioner added, "it would be strenuously opposed by this office."[20] Nevertheless, local business interests remained eager to obtain Oneida land by replacing the Indians' "trust" title to their lands (which barred its sale or taxation) with fee simple titles, a process called "fee patenting." A group within the tribe—that called itself the Progressive Party—supported this idea, but most members opposed it.

The debate over the issuing of fee patents continued through the 1890s and reached a climax in 1906 when a delegation of Progressive Party members traveled to Washington to press its case. As had happened on past occasions when the sale of tribal property was being considered, the local congressman from Green Bay was quick to express his support. In this case the congressman was Edward S. Minor of Sturgeon Bay, the powerful chair of the House Subcommittee on Interior Department Expenditures.[21] The Indian Party immediately spoke up in opposition. The group reminded the Indian Office of the tribe's treaty relationship with the United States, insisting that the United States recognize that its relationship with the Oneidas could not be canceled by a simple shift in political climate or administration policy. "It takes two parties to make a treaty's contract," they insisted, "and it takes two parties to change it, and two parties to lay the treaty aside. And this has never yet occurred in our nation."[22]

Faced with these opposing arguments from within the Oneida community, the Indian Office recommended a middle course. Rather than recommend the wholesale granting of fee patents as the progressives had originally requested, federal officials recommended legislation that would permit action on a case-by-case basis. Commissioner of Indian Affairs

Francis Leupp noted that the Progressives had "receded from the position originally taken" (a wholesale transfer to fee patents) and were willing to leave the issuing of patents to the "discretion of the Secretary of Interior and on the application of any Indian."[23] Leupp's proposal took legislative form in May 1906 when an amendment to the Dawes Act, crafted by the Indian Affairs Committee chair Charles Burke, became law.

The 1906 Burke Act authorized the Interior Department to grant fee patents to any allottee who applied and was judged "competent and capable of managing his or her own affairs." Those who were "incompetent" would be denied U.S. citizenship, and their lands would remain under the protection of the federal government. Together, these provisions shifted the nature of the allotment process away from its original conception (in which allotment would occur slowly and allotted lands would remain protected by federal power for a generation) and toward a new vision that assumed an accelerated pace of allotment and a diminishing (but clear) federal role in the protection of Native resources and people.

But the Burke Act did not satisfy the advocates of fee simple title in Green Bay. In June 1906, barely a month after the passage of the new law, Congress approved an amendment to the Indian Office's annual appropriation bill that broadened the Burke Act's application to the Oneidas. It authorized the secretary of the interior, "in his discretion, to issue a patent in fee to any Indian of the Oneida Reservation." Under this language, Oneidas need not apply for such patents, and the Burke Act's vague standard of "competence" would not be applied.[24] Congressman Minor and his constituents had managed to undermine even the modest protections in the Burke Act. Despite Minor's victory, however, the government agent at Oneida predicted no changes in conditions on the ground. He reassured his superiors that he "did not anticipate a great number" of petitions from tribal members for fee simple land titles.[25] Agent Hart was wrong; the skill of Congressman Minor and his colleagues surprised everyone. Instead of "satisfaction," the archival record reveals that the period immediately following the passage of the 1906 appropriations rider was marked by an onslaught of non-Indian buyers who descended on the reservation. Within three years, nearly half of the reservation's land was covered by fee simple titles, and seven thousand acres of reservation land had been sold.[26]

FORMATION OF TOWNS ON THE RESERVATION

To compound the damage, the Wisconsin state legislature had adopted a statute in 1903 that established the towns of Hobart (in Brown County) and Oneida (in Outagamie County) on land within the boundaries of the Oneida reservation. So long as these two new townships encompassed federal trust land, they remained "paper" entities and had no substance. Once the 1906 budget rider was approved, however, residents of these townships (who included fee patented Oneidas as well as non-Indians) had an incentive to persuade tribal members to remove their land from federal protection.

Once this process began, it snowballed. Local residents—and the white business and political leaders who served them—argued that their young towns' revenues could come only from a fee simple land base. This argument surfaced even in the ongoing contest between the Progressive and the Indian political parties, giving their dispute a new level of local and national visibility. After Cornelius Hill's death, in 1907, the Progressives' most outspoken advocate was Dennison Wheelock, an Oneida lawyer who had been one of the tribe's earliest and most prominent graduates of the famed Carlisle Indian Industrial Training School in Pennsylvania. In the years after Hill's death, Wheelock became a spokesperson for the towns of Hobart and Oneida, urging the Indian Office to use its "influence . . . to induce as many of the Oneida Indians to apply for their patents in fee simple."[27]

Wheelock's advocacy provoked a strong response from the Indian Party. In a petition to the Indian Office filed within weeks of Wheelock's 1909 appeal, Paul Doxtator and ninety-six others protested that "Our nation never agreed to have our Reservation divided into two townships." What is more, they noted that "none was ever authorized by our nation to call for an election for that purpose" and "we are in no way fit to run a town government."[28] The Indian Party also sent Doxtator and his Indian Party ally Amos Baird to Washington to lobby their local representative.

After 1906 the Oneidas were caught in a riptide of economic and political pressure that obscured two foundational truths about the federal government's relations with the tribe. First, despite their internal differences, the Oneidas and the United States had never abandoned the treaty relationship first forged by them in the aftermath of the American Revolution. Second, despite its provisions enabling the division of tribal land, the Dawes Act contained no language terminating the federal government's protective role in Indian affairs. Much of the rhetoric surrounding the allotment law promised that Indian tribes would ultimately disappear, but nothing in the statute defined when or how that event would occur.

In the fall of 1909 the U.S. Senate Committee on Indian Affairs, chaired by Senator (and allotment advocate) Moses Clapp, of Minnesota, visited the Oneida reservation to investigate conditions there. The Progressive and Indian Party leaders testified before the committee, generally repeating the arguments they had made previously, but Indian Party leader Jacob Bread warned that the expansion of Hobart and Oneida raised the prospect that tribal members who had received fee simple titles for their land might soon lose it should they fail to pay Village property taxes. "The way I see it," John Scanadore told the committee, "we are still under the protection of the government and I would like to see the government intercede for us to prevent the separation of personal property from [our] real estate."[29]

The debate over the federal government's role in protecting Oneida allottees' land continued into the 1910s, but none of the Indian Party's concerns slowed the speed with which individual land holdings shifted to fee simple status. In March 1911—almost five years after the 1906 revisions were approved—60 percent of the reservation's lands had shifted from trust protection to fee simple status.[30] During the same years, the Indian Office announced its intention to close the Oneida school. Only the agency policeman and a clerk remained to represent the federal government's continuing relationship to the community.[31]

IMPACTS OF ALLOTMENT IN ONEIDA

As the decade of the 1910s wore on, the Indian Party shifted its focus from fee patenting to concerns regarding the rising tide of land sales and the growing problem of landlessness. Men like Paul Doxtator and his allies worried that the federal government would cease to support them economically and that the tribe would eventually be rendered destitute.[32] While they differed over the wisdom of changing the status of individual land titles and debated the issue of tribal poverty, most Oneidas were united in support of broad tribal causes. The most prominent of those was the effort to obtain monetary damages from the U.S. Court of Claims for violations of past treaties. It was precisely during the decade when fee patenting was at its height that tribal leaders from both major Oneida parties began to see legal claims as an important political cause as well as a possible remedy for tribal poverty. The campaign for a suit before the Court of Claims began at Oneida in 1911, and attorney Dennison Wheelock was one of the group's most outspoken legal advocates.[33]

The debate over whether or not to continue trust patents reached a high point of visibility in 1917 when the remaining Oneida trust allotments were due to expire. More than fifty thousand of the Oneida reservation's sixty-four thousand acres had already been removed from trust status. Most of the fee patented land on Wisconsin reservations—and beyond—was now owned by non-Indians.[34] Even though national reform groups had begun to worry that so many "competent" Native people were losing their land, political support for setting the Indians "free" from federal protection continued. "Our goal is the free Indian," Secretary of the Interior Franklin Lane declared soon after taking office in 1913. Lane declared, "The orphan-asylum idea must be killed in the mind of the Indian and the white man."[35] To press the fee patenting process forward, the secretary appointed a three-person competency commission to review trust allottees at Oneida and determine which of them should be "set free."[36]

The first visit of the competency commissioners to Oneida produced a report on 106 tribal members who still held trust allotments. They concluded that thirty-two individuals in this group were "competent." Of the thirty-two "competents," ten agreed to receive fee patents; the remaining twenty-two refused. In a letter to Commissioner of Indian Affairs Cato Sells, the commissioners recommended that the ten fee patents be approved immediately and the remaining twenty-two applicants be issued their certificates "at the expiration of the trust period" in June. "As to all other allottees," they wrote (a group of at least seventy-four), "the trust period should be extended." The commission made no recommendation regarding the length of that extension or the disposition of approximately five thousand acres of trust land on the reserve that remained in the estates of deceased allottees who had no heirs.[37] Given popular support for rapid fee patenting, the competency commission's initial decisions must have produced a general sigh of relief among Indian Party members. It appeared that a small but significant portion of the Oneidas' 1838 homeland—perhaps 10 percent—would remain in trust beyond the June 12 deadline.

This relief was short-lived. Later in the spring of 1917 the United States declared war on Germany, and the Indian Office announced a national effort to "open" trust lands to increase wartime food production. In May, Senator Robert LaFollette, of Wisconsin, who had corresponded extensively with Dennison Wheelock and other Progressives earlier in his term in office, wrote to Commissioner Sells about the situation at Oneida. Repeating information he had no doubt received from the Green Bay business community, LaFollette reported that 110 allotments on the reservation would remain in trust following the implementation of the March competency commission's report. Combined with the five thousand acres of trust land left by deceased allottees who had no heirs, LaFollette estimated that more than eleven thousand acres of the original tribal estate remained beyond the reach of whites. "It is claimed by those in a position to know," he continued, "that the holders of these trust lands are in every way competent to handle their own affairs and that they refuse to apply for fee patents and favor an extension of the trust period for another ten years solely because of their desire to avoid the payment of real estate taxes." The senator asked that an investigation begin "at once."[38]

The timing of LaFollette's letter was not coincidental. Two weeks earlier, on April 18, an official of the town of Oneida had called the Green Bay attorney Joseph Martin to protest the extension of trust allotments on the reservation. Martin, a former state legislator and a member of the

Democratic Party's national committee, immediately passed the complaint on to Wisconsin's Democratic U.S. Senator, Paul Husting. Husting, in turn, demanded a hearing on the matter at the Indian Office. On May 7, Husting, Dennison Wheelock, and P. W. Silverwood, an attorney representing the towns of Hobart and Oneida, met in Washington with the Indian Office's long-serving chief clerk, C. F. Hauck. At the end of the meeting, Hauck agreed to request a one-year extension of trust allotments at Oneida and to order an immediate investigation of both the five thousand acres of trust land held in the names of deceased tribal members and the remaining trust allotments on the reservation. Three days later, Husting's political rival, the Republican Robert LaFollette, sent his letter to Commissioner Sells.[39] Within days, Secretary of the Interior Lane asked the president to approve a one-year extension of trust patents at Oneida.[40]

On July 24, Commissioner Sells ordered two veteran Indian Office inspectors, James McLaughlin and Frank Brandon, "to make a thorough investigation of the conditions upon the Oneida Reservation in Wisconsin with particular reference to the necessity of a further extension of the period of trust covering allotments made to the Oneida Indians."[41] James McLaughlin's appointment would surely have comforted Senators Husting and LaFollette and the town officials from Hobart and Oneida. Best remembered as the man who had ordered the arrest of Sitting Bull in December 1890, McLaughlin had made a career of riding roughshod over tribal leaders.

McLaughlin and his colleagues met with more than one hundred Oneidas in an open council on August 7. McLaughlin assured the group that he and his colleagues were interested in nothing more than determining the tribe's point of view regarding trust allotments. He claimed to be interested in hearing dissenting views. That dissent surfaced quickly in the wake of the presentations by supporters of fee patenting. Several members of the Indian Party took the floor to oppose removing restrictions on trust land, noting that many Indians who had received fee patents later lost their land. Thomas Cornelius, for example, observed that the tribal members who had acquired full titles "are gone and scattered. . . . They 'aint [*sic*] got no pillow to lay down to rest. . . . I don't call [that] improvement." At the close of the session, the assembly approved a resolution calling for the sale of trust lands left by deceased allottees, provided the proceeds were held in trust for the benefit of the tribe.[42]

DEBATES ON HOW TO MOVE FORWARD

The commission made its recommendations to the secretary of the interior in three separate letters, all dated August 31, 1917. First it discussed the approximately five thousand acres of trust land that had been left in legal limbo by deceased allottees. The commission members acknowledged that children and other descendants of the original allottees were living on these allotments and relying on them for their livelihood, but they recommended that all trust lands be sold.[43] The group then reported on the central source of controversy: the 106 trust allotments that remained on the reservation. The commission recommended extending the trust patent on only eighteen of the more than one hundred cases before it. As Cato Sells later reported, "the commission recommended that the patents be issued to all Indian allottees, living and dead." In May of the following year President Woodrow Wilson affirmed the commission's recommendations, issuing an executive order conferring fee patents on all those listed in the commission's report.[44]

The Indian Party did not accept Wilson's action. In 1918 Paul and Henry Doxtator petitioned to have new inspectors sent to the reservation. The following year Paul Doxtator asked that his fee patent be canceled. In 1920 Louis Christjohn protested the actions taken by state game wardens to restrict him from fishing on the reservation; two years later Chauncy Doxtator made the same complaint. All of these actions were based on the party's consistent opposition to the commission's actions.[45] On another front, several individuals attempted (unsuccessfully) to persuade the Indian Office to continue support for the tribe by extending the life of the agency school.[46] The party's leaders held to a consistent message, but no one in the Indian Office would listen. The agency school closed its doors in 1919.

The most tangible feature of federal guardianship at Oneida in the 1920s was the protection afforded to land that remained under trust title. Once the Oneida school was closed, the Indian Office requested an opinion from the Department of the Interior solicitor regarding the status of the eighty-acre parcel. The solicitor's reply was clear: there was "little or no doubt" that the property "belongs to the Oneida tribe of Indians" and that it could be sold for their benefit.[47] The Indian Office also reviewed the status of lands being taxed by local authorities.

While the federal role in protecting trust land was clear, the extent of the Oneida agency's responsibility to individual tribal members was not. Officials frequently mentioned that fee patented Oneidas were now "free," but the existence of trust protected allotments on the reservation and the presence of a well-defined Indian community there meant that there was still a role for an Oneida agent based in Keshena. That individual reported in 1924 that he "has charge of the affairs of the Menominee, Stockbridge and Oneida Indians so far as these tribes are under the jurisdiction of the United States." Several dozen children from the tribe attended other federal boarding schools each year, principally at Tomah, Wisconsin, and Flandreau, South Dakota.[48]

Despite these shifting circumstances, tribal members at Oneida continued to argue that they belonged to a distinctive community with an ongoing treaty relationship with the United States. In 1928, for example, William Skenandore, one of the twenty-two trust allottees who had refused a fee simple title in 1917, wrote to the Indian Office as "Chairman of the Oneida Indians" and demanded to know under what authority the land surrounding the former Oneida school had been sold. Skenandore cited the Dawes Act's provision that following allotment, "surplus" land would be sold only with the consent of the affected tribe. In a letter addressed to Skenandore, Commissioner Charles Burke rejected the chairman's argument (separate legislation had authorized the sale) but noted that the proceeds of the sale had been distributed to tribal members.[49]

The year following Skenandore's exchange with the commissioner, a Senate committee visited the tribe as part of a broad investigation of conditions on the nation's reservations that had been prompted by growing sympathy for poor and landless Indians. Skenandore—again identifying himself as "chairman" of the Oneida Council—was a principal witness. He told the visiting senators (led by Wisconsin's Robert LaFollette) that he had "several matters" that concerned him. Skenandore declared, "Our constitutional treaty and lawful rights have been disregarded, violated, ignored and trampled upon, caused as you will see by a desperate, despotic, oppressive and adroit bureau, which has reduced the Oneidas from a powerful, loyal, self-supporting, progressive and merciful people, to insignificance." The federal government's relationship to the tribe, he reminded the senators, was "perpetual."[50]

Senator LaFollette and his colleagues did not respond directly to Skenandore's charges. Instead, they concentrated on the immediate problems of bootlegging, health, and education. This exchange between a passionate leader seeking to reaffirm the Oneidas' fundamental treaty relationship to the United States and a group of legislators concerned with budgets and community health captures the nature of the dialogue involving tribal leaders and federal officials in the 1920s. Aware that past policies had produced widespread poverty and landlessness on the reservation, officials at the Indian Office and members of Congress avoided long-term issues and focused instead on immediate complaints. Tribal leaders, in contrast, viewed those problems—education, law enforcement, trespass, taxation—as manifestations of an overarching failure on the part of federal authorities to live up to their guardianship obligations.

Recognition of the Damage Caused by Allotment and the New Deal

By 1932, the participants in the debate over the Oneidas' future seemed frozen in place. Federal officials had come to recognize the cruel consequences of past policies and the damage excessive fee patenting had delivered to the Oneidas. They also accepted that there was a role for the federal government in alleviating these conditions and in serving as the ultimate protector of the tribe. At the same time, they would not respond directly to the appeals from tribal leaders to live up to their guardianship obligations. They insisted that the Indian Office's actions had been legal and that the government's hands were now tied. But Skenandore and his allies remained determined to win recognition for their past treaty relationship and to restore what they viewed as their historic alliance with the United States. They urged the government to view the tribe's predicament in the broad context of their history and of the promises embedded in agreements such as the 1838 treaty. While each side held firmly to its position, the relentless passage of time and the effects of landlessness and poverty continued to weaken the Oneida community, to undermine the tribe's leaders, and to encourage tribal members to take up new lives away from their homeland. Then, suddenly, everything changed.

The "Indian New Deal" launched by federal authorities in 1933 marked a fundamental shift in national policy. Two generations of scholars have debated its origins and significance, but it is clear that the administration of Commissioner of Indian Affairs John Collier brought significant changes.[51] His administration's success derived not only from Collier's administrative skill but also from the wide realization that allotment had failed to reduce Native poverty and that Indian "backwardness" was not the cause of tribal suffering.

John Collier served in the Indian Office from 1933 to 1945, longer than anyone else in American history. His impact on the agency reached from its educational programs to its relationships with other federal departments. The central innovation of his administration, however, was the Indian Reorganization Act (IRA), passed by Congress and signed into law in June 1934. The law ordered an end to allotment and established the legal machinery Indian communities could use to organize new governments and establish business corporations. Within ten years nearly one hundred reservation communities had adopted governing constitutions under the act. The implementation of the Indian Reorganization Act launched a new era of tribal government. The United States was once again the protector—rather than the destroyer—of tribal communities.

John Collier was well aware of the Oneidas' allotment experience. He told a gathering of Indian leaders in March 1934, that while 80 percent of the value of the Indian estate had been lost during the allotment years, the impact of the Dawes Act on different tribes had been variable. At the Oneida reserve, for example, he noted, most tribal members were "landless." And they were not alone. Collier noted that "more than one hundred thousand Indians in the allotment areas have lost all their land down to the last square foot and are entirely landless. . . . The question is," Collier added, "how can this allotment system be changed so as, first, to stop the futile loss of land by Indians; second, to increase the amount of land owned by Indians; and third, protect the rights and equities of those Indians who have not yet lost their land?"[52]

Tribal leaders were eager to participate in the Indian Office's initiatives. During the 1930s federal agencies built new homes and community buildings at Oneida, while tribal members were able to receive economic assistance in the form of food assistance, old-age pensions, subsidies for dependent children, and individual home construction loans. For the first time since their arrival in Wisconsin, the tribe was also able to add to its badly deteriorated land base. During the Collier era the United States restored 1,200 acres of reservation land to Oneida ownership.[53]

INDIAN REORGANIZATION ACT

In February 1934, Collier released an initial draft of what would later become the Indian Reorganization Act. His proposal won broad support from reformers and many Native leaders, but he soon ran into opposition from western congressmen and senators who worried that his proposal was too supportive of tribal culture and too deferential to tribal leaders. To counter this criticism and to generate support for his ideas, Collier organized a series of eleven regional "congresses" with Indian representatives to discuss his proposal. The session to solicit the opinions of Great Lakes communities took place at Hayward, Wisconsin, on April 23 and 24. Collier chaired most of the earlier meetings, but he was not present at Hayward because he had been called back to Washington to meet with legislators negotiating the final language of the reorganization bill. Despite the commissioner's absence, William

Skenandore and the seven other delegates from Oneida were present and eager to discuss the initiative.

When he spoke at Hayward, Skenandore presented a resolution to the gathering that had been adopted by the tribe "assembled in council" the previous month. It declared that the tribe had "felt the spirit of the new deal in the administration of the affairs of the people of the entire country. . . . We believe the best time to encourage a fighter to win is when he is in the midst of battle," the resolution added. "And we are with you, as Oneida Indians, in your struggle . . . to have Congress pass the Indian Rights Bill . . . and should it become a law and a reality, we are sure that, what Abraham Lincoln was to colored people, you are going to be the Abraham Lincoln to the Indians."[54]

The Indian Reorganization Act was approved by Congress two months later, and the Oneidas adopted the law the following December. The tribe then set about writing a tribal constitution and developing a variety of federally sponsored tribal enterprises: home construction, well drilling, agricultural development, and a variety of other "self-help projects."[55] In the course of these events, a new series of tribal political factions arose to compete for office. William Skenandore's supporters eventually lost out to another group headed by Morris Wheelock and Oscar Archiquette (a former Indian Party member). While these rivalries often undermined the unity of the tribe and weakened some tribal initiatives, they underscored the extent to which the onset of the New Deal had revitalized Oneida political life.

CONCLUSION

In the years following the tribe's adoption of the IRA, the Oneidas restored a significant part of their land base and established a stable and increasingly sophisticated tribal government. Their success can be attributed to the century-long efforts of tribal leaders and to the group's remarkable persistence. At its core, the post-1934 history of the Oneida Nation of Wisconsin unfolded as it did because the Oneida people finally taught the federal government to recognize its historic role as the Nation's ally and protector. John Collier understood that lesson. As he noted in 1934, "the answer to the evils of the past and the present is not to abolish the guardianship and responsibility of the federal government but to change it so that it will build up the property of the Indians instead of taking it away."[56]

NOTES

1. D. P. Andrews to Commissioner of Indian Affairs (hereafter CIA), April 28, 1884, Central Classified Files (hereafter CCF), Oneida, 8463-1884, Records Group 75 (hereafter RG 75), National Archives.

2. U.S. Statutes at Large, 24:388; for the differing views of how quickly to allot tribal lands under the Dawes Act, see Hoxie, Frederick E. *A Final Promise: The Campaign to Assimilate the Indians, 1880–1920* (Lincoln: University of Nebraska Press, 2001), 70–73; for a description of its early administration, see Hoxie, *A Final Promise*, 78–80.

3. Elijah Cornelius et al. to Secretary of Interior, January 19, 1887, enclosed with letter to Department of Interior, January 25, 1887, "Support of Bill before Congress, 50776, Doc. 00845.

4. William Parsons to Commissioner of Indian Affairs, August 18, 1887, File 50777, Doc. 00846.

5. Thomas Jennings from the Green Bay Agency to Commissioner of Indian Affairs, September 13, 1887, enclosing petition of Oneida Indians against allotment. NARA, RG75, BIA, E.91, Lttrs. Recd, 1881–1907, Box 419, 24856-1887.

6. James A. Wheelock et al., to Commissioner of Indian Affairs, May 1888, NARA, RG75, BIA, E.91, Lttrs. Recd, 1881–1907, Box 466, 14504-1888.

7. *Milwaukee Sentinel*, February 24, 1888, "To Open Indian Lands," 2, column F.

8. "Indians upon the Oneida Reservation in Wisconsin," May 8, 1888, House of Representatives, 50th Congress, 1st Session, Report No. 2079.

9. Petition of Oneida Leaders, October 16, 1888, in Thomas Jennings to Commissioner of Indian Affairs, November 13, 1888, NARA, RG75, BIA, E.91, Lttrs. Recd., 1881–1907, Box 490, 28447-1888.

10. See Hoxie, *A Final Promise*, chaps. 5 and 6.

11. See Hoxie, *A Final Promise*, chaps. 5 and 6.

12. See Charles E. Cleland, *Rites of Conquest: The History and Culture of Michigan's Native Americans* (Ann Arbor: University of Michigan Press, 1992); Robert E. Bieder, *Native American Communities in Wisconsin, 1600–1960* (Madison: University of Wisconsin Press, 1995); Deward E. Walker, *Conflict and Schism in Nez Perce Acculturation: A Study of Religion and Politics* (Pullman:

Washington State University Press, 1968); Alexandra Harmon, *Indians in the Making: Ethnic Relations and Indian Identities around Puget Sound* (Berkeley: University of California Press, 1998); Emily Greenwald, *Reconfiguring the Reservation: The Nez Perces, Jicarilla Apaches and the Dawes Act* (Albuquerque: University of New Mexico Press, 2002); Christian W. McMillen, *Making Indian Law: The Hualapai Case and the Birth of Ethnohistory* (New Haven: Yale University Press, 2007); Edward Lazarus, *Black Hills, White Justice: The Sioux Nation versus the United States, 1775 to the Present* (New York: HarperCollins, 1991); and Angie Debo, *And Still the Waters Run: The Betrayal of the Five Civilized Tribes* (Princeton: Princeton University Press, 1940).

13. For an extended discussion of Native American leadership during this difficult period, see Frederick E. Hoxie, *This Indian Country: American Indian Activists and the Place They Made* (London: Penguin, 2012), chaps. 5, 6, 7.

14. Commissioner of Indian Affairs to Dana C. Lamb, October 19, 1889, NARA, RG75, BIA, E.96, Lttrs. Sent, Office of Indian Affairs, Land Div., Vol. 189–90.

15. "Protesting Oneida Indians," January 18, 1890, *Washington Post*, 2, Library of Congress, ProQuest Historical Newspaper Database.

16. Department of Interior, Census Office, *Report on Indians Taxed and Indians Not Taxed at the Eleventh Census: 1890* (Washington, D.C.: Government Printing Office, 1894), 620.

17. "Current Events," *Friends Intelligencer*, December 21, 1895, 52, 61.

18. Commissioner of Indian Affairs to Secretary of Interior, March 17, 1898, NARA, RG48, Records of the Secretary of the Interior (hereafter cited as "Rcrds. Secy. of Int."), E.653, Lttrs. Recd., Box 238.

19. On the appointment of the school director as subagent, see "Report of School at Oneida, Wis." in Annual Reports of the Department of the Interior, For the Fiscal Year Ended June 30, 1899, Indian Affairs, Part I, House of Representatives, 56th Congress, 1st Session, Document No. 5, 512; on the agency police, see D. H. George to Commissioner of Indian Affairs, December 26, 1898, NARA, RG75, BIA, E.91, Lttrs. Recd., 1881–1907, Box 1612, 58500-1898. (Interestingly, Agent George praises Captain Archiquette, head of the agency police, who later became a leader of the Indian Party.) Quotation is from Annual Report of the Commissioner of Indian Affairs (hereafter cited as ARCIA), 1895, 326.

20. Acting Commissioner of Indian Affairs to Secretary of Interior, May 1, 1901, NARA, RG48, Rcrds. of Secy. of Int., E.653, Lttrs. Recd., Box 284.

21. Edward S. Minor to Commissioner of Indian Affairs, February 20, 1905, NARA, RG75, BIA, E.91, Lttrs. Recd., 1881–1907, Box 2726, 14641-1905.

22. The Indian Party position was expressed most fully in a petition dated April 1, 1904. Petition of Oneida Members Against Allotment of Land, April 1, 1904, NARA, RG75, BIA, E.91, Lttrs. Recd., 1881–1907, Box 2506, 27502-1904. For *Lone Wolf v. Hitchcock*, see 187 U.S. 553 (1903).

23. Commissioner of Indian Affairs to Secretary of Interior, February 14, 1906, NARA, RG48, Rcrds. Secy. of Int., E.653, Lttrs. Rec., Box 385.

24. James Oberly, "The Dawes Act and the Oneida Indian Reservation," in *The Oneida Indians in the Age of Allotment, 1860–1920*, ed. Laurence M. Hauptman and L. Gordon McLester III (Norman: University of Oklahoma Press, 2006), 193.

25. ARCIA, 1906, 399; and Joseph C. Hart to the Commissioner of Indian Affairs, October 4, 1906, NARA, RG 75, BIA, Lttrs. Recd., 1881–1907, 79780-1906.

26. See "Inspection Report," October 16, 1909, NARA, RG75, BIA, E.121, CCF, 1907–39, Oneida, Box 1, 86325-1-09-030.

27. Dennison Wheelock to the Commissioner of Indian Affairs, January 15, 1909, NARA, RG75, BIA, E.121, CCF, 1907–39, Oneida, Box 26, 8499-09-312.

28. Paul Doxtator et al., to the Commissioner of Indian Affairs, February 1, 1909, NARA, RG75, BIA, E.121, CCF, 1907–39, Oneida, Box 26, 14714-09-312.

29. See "Hearing: Conditions of Indian Affairs in Wisconsin," Hearing at Oneida Reservation, October 2, 1909, Committee on Indian Affairs, 61st Congress, 1st Session (1909), 1097 (Clapp), 1098 (Hill), 1099 (Bread), 1110 (Scanadore).

30. C. F. Hauke to A. S. Baird, March 2, 1911, NARA, RG75, BIA, E.121, CCF, 1907–39, Oneida, Box 26, 16491-09-312.

31. See Cato Sells to Secretary of Interior, May 31, 1919, Charles Davis to Commissioner of Indian Affairs, October 14, 1909, NARA, RG75, BIA, E.121, CCF, 1907–39, Oneida, Box 61, 69348-10-806.

32. Laurence Hauptman, "The Oneidas and the Federal Competency Commission of 1917," in Hauptman and McLester, *The Oneida Indians in the Age of Allotment*, 202.

33. See Dennison Wheelock, "Before the Committee on Indian Affairs," December 18, 1911, NARA, RG75, BIA, E.121, CCF, 1907–39, Box 1, 4809-12-013. The issue of claims seems to have united tribal factions; all could agree that the United States was liable for mismanaging the tribe's finances.

34. See Janet McDonnell, *The Dispossession of the American Indian, 1887–1934* (Bloomington: Indiana University Press, 1991), 8, 101.

35. Lane quoted in McDonnell, *Dispossession*, 92.

36. Franklin K. Lane to Joseph C. Hart, February 3, 1917, NARA, RG48, Rcrds., Secy. of Int., E.749, CCF, 1907–36, Oneida, Allotments, Box 1265, 5-1.

For estimates of remaining trust acreage, see Robert LaFollette to Commissioner of Indian Affairs, May 10, 1917, NARA, RG75, BIA, E.121, CCF, 1907–39, Oneida, 46962-17-313. The national figure for fee patented lands for 1916 is from McDonnell, *The Dispossession*, 101.

37. See O. M. McPherson to Secretary of Interior, March 24, 1917, NARA, RG75, BIA, CCF, 1907–39, Oneida, Box 3, 83738-17-127, Pt. 1. According to the Secretary's February 7 letter a "Captain Trobridge" was the third competency commission member. Hauptman writes that James McLaughlin was the third commissioner. See Laurence M. Hauptman, "The Wisconsin Oneidas and the Federal Competency Commission of 1917," in Hauptman and McLester, *The Oneida Indians in the Age of Allotment*, 206.

38. Robert LaFollette to Commissioner of Indian Affairs, May 10, 1917, NARA, RG75, BIA, E.121, CCF, 1907–39, Oneida, 46962-17-313.

39. The sequence of Martin's, Husting's, and Hauck's actions are described in Hauptman, "Wisconsin Oneidas and the Federal Competency Commission," 210.

40. Franklin K. Lane to President, May 17, 1917, NARA, RG48, Rcrds. Sec. of Int., E. 749, CFF, 1907–36, Oneida Allotments, Box 1265, 5-1.

41. Commissioner of Indian Affairs to Major James McLaughlin and Frank Brandon, July 24, 1917, NARA, RG48, Rcrds. of Secy. of Int., E.749, CFF, 1907–36, Box 1432, 5–6, General, Competent Indians, Pt. 3.

42. See Hauptman, "Wisconsin Oneidas and the Federal Competency Commission," 213–16. Cornelius's statement is on 216.

43. James McLaughlin et al. to Secretary of Interior, August 31, 1917, NARA, RG75, BIA, E.121, CCF, 1907–39, Oneida, Box 3, 83738-17-127, Pt. 2.

44. See second and third letters from James McLaughlin et al. to Secretary of Interior, August 31, 1917,; Cato Sells to Secretary of Interior, September 8, 1917, NARA, RG75, BIA, E.121, CCF, 1907–1939, Oneida, Box 3, 83738-17-127, Pt. 2.; and Executive Order, May 4, 1918, NARA, RG48, Rcrds. Secy. of Int., E.749, CCF, 1907–36, Oneida, Allotments, Box 1265, 5-1. Commissioner of Indian Affairs to Paul Doxtator, July 28, 1919, NARA, RG75, BIA, E.121, CCF, 1907–39, Oneida, Box 44, 60256-19-312.

45. On Christjohn, see Commissioner of Indian Affairs to Edgar A. Allen, April 29, 1920, NARA, RG75, BIA, E.121, CCF, 1907–39, Keshena, Box 32, 33632-20-115; on Doxtator, see Chauncy Doxtator to Commissioner of Indian Affairs, September 25, 1922, NARA, RG75, BIA, E.121, CCF, 1907–39, Keshena, Box 52, 77243-22-155.

46. Paul and Henry Doxtator to Robert M. LaFollette, May 12, 1918, Robert LaFollette Papers; U.S. Library of Congress, Washington, D.C. (Manuscript

Div.) LaFollette Family Collection, Part I, Robert M. LaFollette Sr., 1844–1925, Series B, Box 129, Folder: Indian Affairs File, Oneida, 1912–23, Undated.

47. Solicitor to Secretary of Interior, August 6, 1920, NARA, RG48, Rcrds. Secy. of Int., E.749, CCF, 1907–36, Box 1226, 5-1, Keshena, Tribal Property, Pt. 1.

48. Superintendent W. R. Beyer testified in 1929 that "75–80" Oneida children attended off-reservation federal boarding schools. See Survey of Conditions, July 8, 1929, Library of Congress, Law Library, CIS Microfiche, 71st C., Vol. S 545-2.

49. Commissioner of Indian Affairs to William Skenandore, October 9, 1928, NARA, RG48, Rcrds. Secy. of Int., E.749, CCF, 1907–36, Box 1224, 5-1, Keshena, General.

50. See Survey of Conditions, July 8, 1929, Library of Congress, Law Library, CIS Microfiche, 71st C., Vol. S 545-2. Skenandore's testimony is reproduced on 918–1930.

51. The literature on the New Deal reforms is very large. Major works include Kenneth R. Philp, *John Collier's Crusade for Indian Reform, 1920–1954* (Tucson: University of Arizona Press, 1977); Graham D. Taylor, *The New Deal and American Indian Tribalism: The Administration of the Indian Reorganization Act* (Lincoln: University of Nebraska Press,1980); Vine Deloria Jr. and Clifford Lytle, *Nations Within: The Past and Future of American Indian Sovereignty* (Austin: University of Texas Press, [1984] 1998); F. P. Prucha, *The Great Father* (Lincoln: University of Nebraska Press, 1986); and Paul Rosier, *Serving Their Country: American Indian Politics and Patriotism in the Twentieth Century* (Cambridge, MA: Harvard University Press, 2009).

52. Vine Deloria Jr., ed., *The Indian Reorganization Act* (Norman: University of Oklahoma Press), 28.

53. See Robert E. Ritzenthaler, "The Oneida Indians of Wisconsin," *Bulletin of the Public Museum of the City of Milwaukee* 19, no. 1 (November 1950): 14–15.

54. See Deloria, *The Indian Reorganization Act*, 387–88, 397–98; the members of the Oneida delegation are listed on p. 401.

55. See Laurence Hauptman, *The Iroquois and the New Deal* (Syracuse: Syracuse University Press, 1981), 70–87, 82. Skenandore became an opponent of the IRA, largely because the new council reduced his influence and he continued to prefer a focus on treaty rights. See Hauptman, *The Iroquois and the New Deal*, and William Skenandore to Commissioner of Indian Affairs, December 20, 1934, NARA, RG75, E.1011, BIA, Rcrds. of the Indian Organization Division, re: Wheeler-Howard Act, Box 4.

56. Deloria, The Indian Reorganization Act, 27.

—◠—

CHAPTER 3

Evolution of a Nation

WILLIAM GOLLNICK

KEY TERMS IN THIS CHAPTER
- Treaty
- Intergovernmental agreement

Onʌkwi uskah ʌwatu yukatnikullala. May our minds become as one. I share the words in this chapter as a gift to the reader. I trust that by providing an understanding of our experience we can then come collectively to a more reasoned and informed understanding of how we arrived at this point in history, in this place, and where we may go from here.

The Oneida, onʌyote aka or People of the Standing Stone, are known as unkwehuweh. There is not a direct translation for that word, but it engenders the concepts of original people, authentic people, real people. Our ancestors made treaties with the Dutch in the 1530s and later with the British and the Colonies and ultimately with the United States during the subsequent three-hundred-year period. We are the original people of this land.

"Hotinosaunee" is our word for what is known to most as the Iroquois Confederacy. Our homeland is basically what is now the state of New York. The Hotinosaunee nations were represented by the Grand Council, or fifty chiefs. The Oneida had nine of those chiefs. When the Tuscarora joined the Confederacy in the early 1700s, they sat with our chiefs, and their voices were represented by our leaders. The Hotinosaunee were thereafter known as the Six Nations.

The Grand Council was a forum for addressing the needs of the Hotinosaunee people. Issues of each nation that did not extend beyond its borders or tribal members were left to that member nation to resolve. This concept, which became part of America's discussions of states' rights, was not lost on Benjamin Franklin, who was the liaison for the Albany Congress. He marveled at the model in praxis as a government of the people.

As Franklin was learning from us about upper and lower governmental bodies and checks and balances, he also built relationships that served America well. When the Revolution was gaining support from the colonials, the Hotinosaunee attempted neutrality. This was a war that our people saw as a war between brothers. This was not our fight.

It was clearly recognized that the Hotinosaunee could be a significant ally . . . or a significant enemy. Both of the brothers exerted pressure on our people. We had to choose with whom we would side. Oneidas and Tuscaroras chose to fight alongside the Colonies. We fought the British at Oriskany and brought food to Washington's starving army at Valley Forge. Our lands in New York were to be protected forever for our service.

History usually accounts for outcomes with the victors retaining the spoils of war. Although we had fought and died and prevailed with our American allies, we were still Indians, and when the leadership wanted Indian lands and resources, we, along with most other "eastern tribes," were being forced west. "Forever" lasted until Andrew Jackson and his followers committed to moving all American Indians west of the Mississippi.

Our relatives to the south, the Cherokee, took another path. Gold had been found on their lands, and America wanted that, too. Unlike the majority of Hollywood movie plots, the Cherokee didn't attack the fort or the wagon train; the Cherokee went to court. Three significant cases came to shape the intergovernmental relationship between the federal government and the tribal governments. What was evolving was a jurisdictional relationship that would become known as federal Indian Law.

Johnson v. M'Intosh, *Cherokee Nation v. Georgia*, and *Worcester v. Georgia* limited anyone other than the United States from buying Indian lands, defined the tribal nations as domestic dependent nations, and clarified that Indian governments had jurisdiction over their people on their lands.[1] Those principles continue to this day. What occurred from that period until the 1970s was the cause of so many of the contemporary disagreements, misunderstandings, and upheavals.

The 1820s saw us relocating to Wisconsin. We entered into a treaty with the Menominee, with the United States as an observer. We agreed to share in the Menominee lands rather than acquiring a separate parcel. Some of the Menominee disagreed with the terms after a few years and asked the United States to intervene. The Menominee's lands were dramatically reduced and our final treaty with the United States defined our 65,430-acre reservation in 1838, ten years before Wisconsin entered the Union.[2]

In 1869 the last Indian treaty was ratified. In 1871 Congress acted to end treaty-making with the Indian nations. The process had resulted in political stress. The Executive Branch initiated the negotiations, and the Senate would be called upon to consider and ultimately ratify the terms. That would then engage the House, which would have to find the money and/or arrange for the exercise of authority to achieve the terms of the agreement. If the House had to find the money, it wanted to be part of the negotiation. The preceding treaties were unaffected, but thereafter, the agreements with Indian tribes would be negotiations within policy and not treaty negotiations.

In the late 1870s, an army officer, Richard Henry Pratt, developed the idea of taking Indian children from their tribes and families and educating them in federally run institutions. These schools had very restricted curricula and very militaristic structures. The students were not allowed to speak their languages or participate in any cultural or traditional activities. They were being reprogrammed. Their hair was cut. The boys wore cut-down military uniforms. The girls all got gingham dresses. They were trained to be farmers or welders and domestics. America was reprogramming Indians to become a class of blue-collar or no-collar workers and cooks and cleaning ladies. The process cut multiple ways. Pratt's catchphrase, which became the impetus for this process, was "Kill the Indian, save the man." If Indians could be turned into brown (or red) white people, then they would not need to be killed. Maybe they could even be absorbed into the American melting pot.

American Indians were not permitted to learn about themselves or their history. They would return home after years of institutional life and barely know their families. They didn't fit in. They couldn't speak their languages. That was the intent of these schools. At the same time, all American children were being educated via curricula that simply excluded American Indian content. Indians weren't allowed to know; everyone else just didn't know to ask. The result was the same. Indian rights were simply being allowed to drift into some never-never land. Textbook references to Indians ceased after about 1850, and all things Indian were viewed as from long ago or anachronistic.

States were exercising jurisdiction that they didn't have. Tribes didn't have the resources to fund the services that were within their jurisdiction. The Oneida had a Bureau of Indian Affairs (BIA) agent who attended every General Tribal Council meeting to report that there was no money to do what needed to be done. That was the federal trust authority that was being exercised. Tribal leaders were not appropriately prepared to exercise their governmental authority and jurisdiction, and American Indians were about 500 percent behind the national average in postsecondary education.

America's civil rights debates were debates between Black and white Americans. The majority of Americans had no idea that Indian issues even continued. In 1970 a *Time* article spoke to the First American becoming the last American in every socioeconomic category.

Before there were notebooks, smartphones, and internet access, people learned about daily or weekly events via the newspapers. The reporting provided snapshots and cursory information to the reader. What today is referred to as "deep dives" or investigative and more comprehensive reporting fell to magazines like *Time*. They dedicated the staff and editorial priorities to fleshing out the stories associated with current events.

Time magazine's continuing coverage reported on Indian women being sterilized after the Family Planning Services and Population Research Act of 1970.[3] Twenty-five percent or more of the childbearing-age Indian women were sterilized in just a six-year period. An organization known as AIM, the American Indian Movement, evolved and became another voice of America's Indigenous People, particularly the youth. In 1973 it became very visible with the takeover of Wounded Knee on the Pine Ridge reservation.

The Menominee were fighting for restoration after having been terminated in a seven-year process that had begun in the 1950s. They were becoming active on a number of fronts. In 1975 a group of mostly Menominee tribal members took over a vacated complex known as the Alexian Brothers novitiate.[4] It was a site on lands near their reservation, and, in the logic of the time, vacant property was being reclaimed by Native Americans. The activists were not formal representatives of the tribal government but rather were a group of younger tribal members who wanted to raise awareness of political and socioeconomic issues. After a couple months of occupation, they were arrested and jailed.

Marge Stevens, an Oneida woman and mother of Ernie Stevens Jr., the current chair of the National Indian Gaming Association, joined with other parents and began the Indian Community School in her Milwaukee residence. The American Indian Movement occupied a vacant Coast Guard station on the shore of Lake Michigan, and negotiations between Indian families and local officials led to permission for the use of the station as a school as long as it was performing educational purposes.

Indians Now on the Radar

The primary issue contributing to the incredible unrest in the 1970s was the hunting and fishing rights of the Ojibwe.[5] In the 1850s, six bands of the Lake Superior Chippewa had ceded approximately one-third of the state of Wisconsin to the United States while preserving the rights to hunt, fish, and gather in the ceded territory. Somewhere along the way, Wisconsin decided it had jurisdiction, and the rights of the Ojibwe were relegated to a dusty shelf with the other elements of Native American history and knowledge.

Elders who had spoken for generations were now joined by younger tribal members who were pursuing education, many actually benefiting from the federal Indian Education Act of 1972.[6] Information was also traveling by Moccasin Telegraph. Word of mouth was broadcasting ideas in informal ways. Former Oneida chairman Jerry Danforth might refer to that as "lightning across the rez," Suddenly, Indian people were gaining access to information that had been restricted. They learned that they had rights that, unless exercised, could potentially be permanently taken away.

Imagine . . . a light at the end of the tunnel! Tribal rights and treaty terms were going to be honored. Tribes could begin to climb out of the depths of their poverty and determine a course for their future and future generations. They were committed to exercising those rights—and then came the backlash.

The Indian Wars weren't over. Suddenly the rules of engagement were changing in significant ways.

Non-Indians were confused and affronted that Indians were challenging the status quo. Many tribal members too were uncertain about the state of their authority, the power they held as members of an Indian nation. How could they enhance the status of their people? Remember, Indians weren't allowed to learn about themselves. And yet, as Pratt had lamented, the Indians always returned to the blanket (returned to their people and ways). Not everyone knew what was on the horizon but there was a flurry of activity, and the impetus for change required educating about the true conditions and circumstances. Something new was coming, but what would that something look like?

The Oneida had reached for any potential legal opportunity to develop a meaningful budget that could support services and development, but the restrictions were many. What land the tribe owned was in federal trust and could not be used for collateral. The tribe had an annual budget in three figures and relied mostly on lease payments for homesites and agricultural leases for income. The federal government was not meeting its obligations, and we were woefully behind in education and preparation to assert the type of comprehensive governance that was needed. Senator Daniel Inouye of Hawaii, co-chair of the Senate Committee on Indian Affairs, often spoke of the more than four hundred treaties with the Indian nations that had been broken by the United States. He was committed to having America recognize the treaties and uphold the honor of the country. Lofty, but absent resources, there was a long way to go.

Were we simply all residents of our reservation and able to function in the best version of how a tribe might pursue its planning and make its decisions for the common welfare, we would have seen a monumental task. Nation building! The Indian Reorganization Act of 1934 had been analyzed and considered, and a new constitution had been adopted by us in 1936.[7] Evolving from a unicameral body with a very limited structure to a comprehensive and innovative government capable of meeting the diverse, deep-seated, and evolving challenges faced by our people forty years on was a huge challenge. In a vacuum it would have been an enormous undertaking. But we were not in a vacuum.

SHARED BOUNDARIES AND MIXED POPULATION

With many of the residents of our reservation being non-Indians, frictions arose as the tribe moved forward. Did these Indians find a treaty in a tin can in someone's back yard? How could the United States honor their status? Didn't we beat them in the Indian wars? What gives them the right to land in our counties? They're not going to govern me! The Oneida were blessed with their own chapter of an organization called Equal Rights for Everyone that made these and numerous other public claims.

The policies that encouraged us to attend BIA schools, the relocation initiatives and policies that encouraged us to move to the cities, the loss of much of our land within the reservation boundaries due to vacillating federal policies that alternatingly honored and disregarded the terms of treaty or law made everything unclear. We had good, dedicated, honorable elected tribal leaders, but there were many questions about how we would, how we could proceed. We also had detractors at every turn.

The tribe's capacity to perform the array of responsibilities assigned to it was dramatically hindered by a lack of resources and the depth of research necessary to fully develop, codify and implement a truly comprehensive array of services. The Business Committee was the body authorized to govern when the General Tribal Council was not in session.[8] It met regularly and used its knowledge and experience to render decisions and determine how best to meet obligations and commitments. It did the best it could and was generally respected by the tribal members, but, absent budgets and staff, how would the government meet all the demands?

The role of government is to serve its constituency. It exists to provide services and assistance, education, the advancement of opportunity, and so on. When one thinks of a tribal government, it usually involves other cultural traditional elements, values, and traditions, The undercurrent of cultural values and traditions were of import to those working in Oneida in the 1970s. The intent was to carry out the governmental authority of the tribe while developing a framework and guidance for the exercise of traditions blended with the evolution of the tribe's role as a government and partner with the federal government in the growth of the Oneida tribe.

In the 1960s, the Oneida's General Tribal Council (GTC) meetings were still conducted primarily in the Oneida language. The GTC was composed of the resident members of the reservation who were twenty-one years of age and older. Those who had left the reservation through the federal Relocation Program or otherwise could come home to participate in the elections and other meetings. The federal initiatives to get Indians off the reservations had managed to destabilize many tribes, but the connections were not broken.

When President John F. Kennedy declared America's intention to put a man on the moon, scientists began an incredibly dedicated initiative to make that happen. In the mid-1960s they believed they could send a man to the moon but were unsure about whether they could get him back. Renowned Lakota author Vine Deloria quipped that they should send an Indian to the moon on Relocation . . . and he'd find his own way back.

The Oneida now had many non-Indians residing within the reservation boundaries and different statuses of land ownership. As a matter of federal law, once established, an Indian reservation continues to exist until or unless the federal government by a purposeful act diminishes or disestablishes it. The feds had clearly not done that with the Oneida, but many then living in the community wanted to make the tribe's status go away. Most Americans did not understand treaty law. They didn't understand that Indian nations had made treaties that made them allies and that defined terms and obligations. Most thought that our history was the cowboys and Indians of Hollywood.

The American Indian reality is not only different from Hollywood's dramatizations; it is also different from the reality of all other people in America. All Americans except Indians came from somewhere else. All others have a place in the world that is theirs, where their languages are spoken, their cultures are practiced, their ancestors are buried. American Indians have their reservations. If the reservations are taken, we cease to exist. The unkwehuweh will be no more. We cannot allow that. We must persevere.

The year 1975 brought the Indian Self-Determination and Education Assistance Act.[9] The BIA was being downsized, and the savings would now be made available to the tribal governments to carry out the services that the feds had been obligated to address but seldom did successfully. Tribes would now be required to report to the feds on their success in the provision of services but could adapt their approaches to achieve the federal mandates with culturally sensitive approaches.

As tribes including the Oneida were now not only complying with federal laws but also making laws that represented their culture and jurisdiction, they were also recognizing that the development in Indian country was indeed progress but that "Indian Self-Determination," which was the umbrella under which the growth was authorized, was a misnomer. Tribes weren't self-determining if they were simply carrying out federal mandates. To be truly self-determining, the tribes would need to be self-sustaining. Federal programs meant federal restrictions and obligations. For tribes to be self-determining, they would need to generate jobs and create a vision of the future that they could somehow control.

One of our most revered Oneida tribal chairs was a man named Purcell Powless. I recall how he would become frustrated that Indian country was being expected to shift direction with changes in the D.C.

political winds, and he would lament how "the tail is wagging the dog." As we committed to rebuilding our nation, we needed to plan for more than two years or four years and needed to ground our planning on the needs and aspirations of our people. Federal budget to federal budget and federal priority to priority was antithetical to a nation redefining aspirations for seven generations.

An entity that doesn't change dies. The values that we hold dear can be sustained, but how we honor them, how we preserve them, how we integrate them into our daily lives and respect them will evolve. How would we address the housing needs, educational needs, employment needs of our people? To what end? What should we expect the Nation to look like as we defined our goals and plotted our steps to achieve them? How would we balance the priority of environmental preservation with land use policies that could meet the Nation's residential and economic needs?

People who plan for counties, villages, towns, or cities have an established infrastructure, employment base, services array, and most other attributes of government. As they plan, they largely work around the edges. They add to or modify what exists. Indian country was challenged to basically grow from ground zero.

Some non-Indians owned stores on the reservation. One at Chicago Corners, Mass's, was a very small but classically stocked general store with everything from milk to hardware. It primarily served people at "the other end." Schroeder's and Morgan's were groceries, and Morgan sold some homemade bakery. These two stores were more central to the reservation. Beyond that, the rez had gas stations and churches.

A federal agency, the Department of Housing and Urban Development (HUD), made grant funds available to tribes to conduct planning activities. That was a reasoned first step. A plan was a good thing, but without any resources, it was not going to get you very far. The Oneida employed three of its elected officers as HUD 701 planners.

Without a viable economic sector, there were no jobs. Beyond agriculture, predominantly dairy, the best opportunities were at the paper mills. The mills offered the best salaries and benefits for blue-collar workers. They focused their hiring on the friends and family of their employees, however, and very few Oneidas had that entrée. The reservation was just the community on the border of Green Bay where the poor Indians lived.

The Oneida reservation was arguably gerrymandered in every way conceivable—multiple counties, townships, even school districts. The ten-by-twelve-mile reservation was in six school districts, and not one actually sited a facility within the reservation boundaries. Our children were distinct minorities in each district, and there was no central gathering place within the rez for our young people to come together. We needed to work on that.

All communities have occasional needs for police. Local law enforcement was provided by the counties, and each half of the reservation was served by one of the two counties that divided it. Obviously on the border, response times were slow, and, to be candid, many officers seemed uncomfortable to be on the reservation. Two Oneidas were in law enforcement, one on staff in each of the counties. We convinced them to take on the challenge of establishing our own police force. They became our first two sworn officers. Our force began with well-trained, experienced officers who were based locally and could respond timely to issues as they arose—a great start.

We were providing services that expanded our capacity while not increasing the local fiscal obligation. We were adding to the local law enforcement, and by negotiating agreements with the county sheriffs, we had our officers cross-deputized so that it was clear that they could engage in mutual aid as requested and enforce the tribal, state, and local laws and ordinances. Win, win.

Beginning steps in education focused on preschool, and particularly early childhood education. The Great Lakes Intertribal Council, on behalf of all Wisconsin tribes, received a federal grant to fund Head Start sites on each of the reservations. This was an early success.

In the mid-1970s we continued educational initiatives. We developed an Oneida Language Project with funding from the U.S. Department of Education. We grew it to seventeen teachers instructing 350 children in four school districts in three years. We hired Oneidas to serve as home school coordinators, liaisons for children and parents with the public schools. They performed counseling, advising, tutoring, and advocacy functions.

Our language program contributed to an early model of how we could proceed. Not yet having our tribal school, we negotiated time slots in the public school day for our children to be taught by our program personnel on site at the schools. This intergovernmental agreement showed how we could cooperate, and we also demonstrated that this type of agreement need not be a zero-sum game. We were drawing upon new funds to make this happen. We were bringing revenue and opportunity to the area at no local expense.

Developing health support was another vitally important initiative. Our people were not healthy. Heart disease, diabetes, high blood pressure, and other maladies were commonplace. Without a viable employment base, few could afford insurance, and health care was something that one pursued as a last resort. People would go to the ER when a problem was unbearable. We needed to work on that, too.

As we did our planning, we began to look at critical success factors. One of our health-related priorities was to reduce the number of amputations. This was something personal to me. My grandmother had both legs amputated and was legally blind as a result of diabetes. Sadly, her experience was not atypical. We engaged with the Indian Health Service and negotiated the foundational agreement that began our clinic—another significant step toward the Oneidas' ability to meet the needs of its constituents.

Because the title to Indian land is held by the feds, it is not taxable by state or local authorities. Services on reservations ensured by treaty or federal law are the obligation of the federal government to finance. If the feds didn't and the tribe couldn't, any assistance that was rendered came from the counties.

Other opportunities arose that the tribe pursued. Social service programs were critically needed. As the tribe was able to secure federal funding, it addressed the needs of its people and diminished the need for county staff and services. Diminished local expenditures and expanded services—win, win.

Enter the Village of Hobart

There were only a couple of paved county roads that traveled through the rez; most roads were gravel. The ditches and surrounding areas were generally grey in the summer as the dust clouds would rise behind the cars and settle around the roadways. Long stretches would become "washboard" as rez traffic and farm equipment created ruts and potholes. Another project.

We candidly felt that roads would be a logical mutually beneficial opportunity for the area. The Reservation Roads program works with tribes to construct and maintain the roads and bridges within Indian country. In order to have the roads placed on the inventory for funding, the tribes would need to demonstrate that the roads were theirs. By securing agreements from the various municipalities within the reservation, it would have been possible for us to receive federal funds, and those costs could have been removed from the local tax base. All residents and others traveling through the reservation would have benefitted at no local cost. Hobart, a community entirely within the boundary of the reservation, objected and instead pursued a course to become a village. It did an end run on the state policies and got an authorization slipped into a budget bill. As a village it would have greater authority than a town and more leverage to tax and challenge the tribe's authority regarding municipal services. Reducing its mill rate was less important than competing with the Oneida Nation for power. The Village was going to show the Oneidas that it could do what the tribe did . . . and it was willing to make the local taxpayers pay for it. Lose, lose.

Hobart's town chairman was a man named Len Teresinski, who hired an administrator named Joe Helfenberger. The Town Board under Teresinski was decidedly adversarial. Our experience was clear that anything supported by or advocated by the tribe would draw fire. Joe was a more even-keeled type who was obligated to follow orders, but he also understood the legitimacy of many of the tribe's positions. I recall how the tribe had contributed funds to the town to improve some roads that the town would not turn over to the tribe. Joe came sheepishly forward with a request that we allow him to use the funds to improve the center of the road and not the part that touched tribal land. I told him that if that was permitted by his codes that he could do so. It was not, and the town had to fix "our" part of the road as well.

Hobart elected a new Village Chair. Rich Heidel courted the tribe and expressed his desire to work cooperatively. The balance of the old guard continued on the board, and Heidel was soon persuaded to work through confrontation rather than cooperation. He became the face of the initiative to bring in a woman named Elaine Willman.

Refuse pickup was another service provided by the tribe that caused consternation among members of the Village Board. If Oneida had that service, Hobart had to provide it as well. So Hobart contracted another provider to pick up for the non-Oneida residents. The trucks cover the same routes on different days and the taxpayers get to cover that as well . . . lose, lose again.

Hobart was quite taken with the anti-Indian agitator Elaine Willman. Ms. Willman claimed she had Indian blood, but all of her initiatives attempted to disrupt the federal–Indian relationship. She headed an organization called Citizens Equal Rights Alliance, and Hobart brought her out from the West Coast to educate the residents about how to fight Indians. In fact, Hobart hired her to become the town's "Indian Liaison." She was in her glory. No more scrambling for donations; now she had a governmental budget and could hire attorneys to address Indian rights issues across the country. Although she focused on suing the Oneida, her broader agenda pulled the Village into court on a country-wide scale.

Heidel, beyond his personal legal faux pas, and Willman pursued things like removing the tribe's no-trespassing signs, placed for safety reasons on an undeveloped future site of a walking trail. Willman sent her staff out to pick up the Nation's signs. When we challenged Ms. Willman on the legal authority of her actions, she said that Helfenberger had left instructions to take down the signs when spring came. The Village returned the signs to us. It would have had responsibility for any accident that might have occurred when it pulled down our signs. Another taxpayer liability . . . could have been a bigger lose, lose.

Oneida Nation Continues Plans
to Move Forward

Oneida, for years, had reacquired lands within the rez. The purposes for the acquisitions varied, and the intent was in some cases to simply reestablish our base. Some purchases were to restore wetlands and for other environmental purposes; some were for residential or economic development. One of our first initiatives was to develop a nursing home. When we began our planning, many of our elders spoke Oneida as a first language, and we wanted to provide an environment where they could interact and converse comfortably. The BIA's school initiatives were finally taking their toll, and there were fewer Oneida speakers each year. Oneida's nursing home, named after a wonderful firebrand named Anna John, functioned as a mainstream state-licensed facility. The facility had space and included non-Oneida residents. Hobart, of course, needed to develop a nursing home as well.

I recall how there was to be a high-capacity gas line to run from southern Wisconsin to a terminus north of the rez. The first choice, of course, was to run the length of the reservation, where the land was the least developed. It was the least developed because the tribe's priority was to preserve the land. As the tribe now had gaming, it was allocating millions of dollars to land acquisition and was committed to preserving the natural environment. We negotiated with those advocating the siting of the pipeline and offered that if they would meet the tribe's annual allocation for the preservation of lands we would grant an easement. They found that excessive and went around the reservation. Our residents, Indian and non-Indian, were pleased, those around us much less so.

The desire to prepare the next generation of leaders contributed to the development of the onʌyotea ka tsiʔ thuwatilihunya niht, the Oneida Tribal School. Literally, The Oneidas, where they teach them. I recall buying our first school bus, and it arrived with the school's name on its side. Locals complained that there was probably something inappropriate written there, and we had to submit a letter to the State on Oneida letterhead that verified the legitimacy and correctness of the writing.

We began with an approach that would serve K-8, and our plan was to expand a year at a time over the next four years to logically stay with a group of students as we built out our plan and refined our curriculum. We were unable to do so as each year's growth would have required a completely independent review, and any shift in federal priorities could have truncated the process. We opted to pursue the high school all at one time. We were successful, but the preparation work was extremely demanding.

Our intention was to develop a unique and traditionally grounded institution with the capacity to instruct all topics in the Oneida language. This was beyond our ability to achieve. Oneida was taught as another subject at the school and could not become the medium for instruction. We didn't have the personnel or written curricular resources to make that happen. We committed, however, to a curriculum that would teach our children about themselves, about our world, and about our history. We committed to teaching our children about math, science, social studies, and a comprehensive array of content so that they were prepared to understand the world as proud Oneida people prepared to stand with all others academically and politically.

The purpose of that foundation and the intention of the tribal government was to grow, develop, create, problem-solve, innovate, preserve, and strengthen the Nation. The goals included enhancing language and cultural practice in a modern world. Committees of members with cultural knowledge, academic knowledge, vision, curiosity, and dedication came together to challenge and advance their ideas and propose innovations.

Evolving from an impoverished community to a nation with the capacity to define its future was a little ethereal. The ether was tempered by Willman's initiatives. Local people were pleased with the services provided by our police force. So Hobart had to create its own . . . and then attempt to get the counties not to dispatch to our officers because the people of Hobart wanted only their officer to be summoned. We held community meetings in the interest of educating local residents about how the tribe's initiatives were beneficial to the area. Willman used those meetings as a guide to create a road map for what had to be challenged by the Village. One step forward, two steps back.

The conservancy on the north edge of the rez was not in trust and the Village exercised eminent domain to enable it to build a remarkably serpentine road that places much under asphalt. The Village decided it needed to paint a water tower with the name "Hobart" displayed prominently displayed right after Oneida purchased the adjoining golf course. It of course had to store its equipment on the cart paths for the weeks it took to complete the project. It also said the former owner didn't own and therefore couldn't convey the restrooms on the course and therefore our patrons couldn't use them. You get the picture . . . on and on.

Undeterred, the tribe pursued numerous avenues. Social service programs were critically needed. Those were services that, absent the tribe's resources, the counties would need to provide. The tribe developed its own services, provided by its own employees, and collaborated with the counties to optimize the services to those within the reservation and surrounding counties. Intergovernmental agreements and formal and informal collaborative initiatives laid a foundation for those of good will. Willman and company continued to file law suits at every turn, but those initiatives got old.

CONCLUSION

Willman moved on, and the last I heard she was trying to foment disruption among tribes and surrounding communities in Montana. In a piece with Samantha Bee, Willman acknowledged that people call her "KKK," "bigot," and other names.[10] But she assured Bee that she would not be going away; she had to stand up to the Indians' use of sharia law. Although I know of no Muslim American Indian nations, I know that Willman will undoubtedly say that she has heard of one somewhere. It must be so . . . she's a Village official.

Hobart's jack booting caused Brown County to retreat from the intergovernmental agreements negotiated with the tribe, but they have since been reinstated. Hobart continues to lose most of its suits against the tribe, and its last initiative was expected to go to the U.S. Supreme

Court. The Village has been dedicated for years to diminishing the authority of the tribe. The opportunity was there to petition the High Court for certiorari, but Hobart chose not to. For most of the Village's suits, the United States and the State of Wisconsin joined with the tribe in opposition to Hobart's positions. To my way of thinking, putting *Hobart v. Oneida* or *Hobart v. Wisconsin* or Hobart against the World has been their claim to fame. I believe that the idea of having *Hobart v. Oneida* go in favor of the tribe and having Hobart forever stand for the sovereignty of all Indian nations gave them pause.

The Oneida Nation perseveres. Our seventeen thousand tribal members have a home, a place that is theirs.

NOTES

1. 21 U.S. 543 (1823); 30 U.S. 1 (1831); 31 U.S. 515 (1832).

2. Treaty with the Oneida, 7 Stat. 566, February 3, 1838.

3. B. Theobald, "The Native American Women Who Fought Mass Sterilization," *Time*, December 5, 2019, https://time.com/5737080/native-american -sterilization-history/.

4. See P. Srubas, "It Gained National Attention during a 34-Day Armed Standoff in 1975. Now, This Dilapidated Gresham Mansion Is for Sale," *Green Bay Press Gazette*, March 7, 2020, https://www.greenbaypressgazette.com/in -depth/news/2020/03/04/gresham-novitiate-property-site-historic-1975-meno minee-takeover-sale-2-million/4765699002/.

5. See R. Whaley and W. Bresette, Walleye Warriors: An Effective Alliance against Racism and for the Earth (Philadelphia: New Society, 1994).

6. Part A, Title IX of the Education Amendments of 1994 (Public Law 103-382).

7. 25 U.S. Code ch. 14, subch. V (1934) §§461 et seq. See Francis Skenandore, "William Skenandore," in *The Oneida Indian Experience: Two Perspectives*, ed. Jack Campisi and Laurence M. Hauptman (Syracuse: Syracuse University Press, 1988), 126–30.

8. Oneida Nation Constitution, accessed December 20, 2021, https://onei da-nsn.gov/wp-content/uploads/2018/05/2015-06-16-Tribal-Constitution.pdf.

9. 25 U.S.C. ch. 14.

10. P. Weber, "Samantha Bee Looks at Tribal Sovereignty and Its Strange Array of Powerful Enemies," *The Week*, June 21, 2016, https://theweek.com/ speedreads/631404/samantha-bee-looks-tribal-sovereignty-strange-array-power ful-enemies.

CHAPTER 4

Condemnation

Resisting Development on Nation-Owned Land

REBECCA M. WEBSTER

KEY TERMS IN THIS CHAPTER

- Condemnation/eminent domain
- Alienation
- Tribal sovereign immunity
- Allotment
- Fee patents

The Oneida Nation has a long history of reacquiring land on its reservation. Beginning in 1977 and continuing to 2010, the tribe's governing body passed a total of eleven government resolutions expressing a commitment to repurchase all available land on the Oneida reservation.[1] Since then there have been various efforts and strategies to reacquire land. One of the goals associated with these plans is to control development on the reservation and to protect environmentally sensitive areas.

The Nation's reacquisition of land resulted in a lawsuit regarding the Village of Hobart's authority to condemn two parcels of land owned by the Nation on the Oneida reservation. One parcel was in a proposed village industrial park. The other parcel was in an environmentally sensitive area of the reservation threatened with development. When the Nation purchased the first parcel and objected to village efforts to condemn land for a road, the Village sued tribal officials in state court. Ultimately, the Nation sued the Village in federal court to challenge the

Village's claimed authority to condemn tribal fee land. At the heart of the issue here was whether federal law allowed condemnation of tribally owned fee land on the reservation.

In 2008, the United States District Court for the Eastern District of Wisconsin ruled in favor of the village and determined that the Village may condemn and levy special assessments against previously allotted fee land owned by the Nation, unless and until the land is placed into trust. The court declared that "Land is either exempt from state law, or it is not."[2] In 2008 the Brown County Circuit Court dismissed the Village's state court case due to resolution of the issues in the federal court decision.

BACKGROUND

Allotment Acts and the Indian Reorganization Act

In 1887 Congress passed the General Allotment Act (GAA), which was the result of a compromise between legislators who were motivated by the plight of Indians on reservations and others who wanted to get rid of reservations and get their hands on the land.[3] Pursuant to the Allotment Act, the president of the United States was authorized to select Indian reservations to be allotted. Those reservations were then surveyed; individual tribal members received title to parcels of land in the form of trust patents, and the land was not subject to taxation or alienation. The land was to remain in trust for a period of twenty-five years. Beginning in 1892, tribal members on the Oneida reservation began to receive their trust patents.

After the twenty-five-year trust period, the tribal members were to receive fee patents for their land. The land would then become taxable and alienable, meaning the tribal members could sell or mortgage their land. Non-Indians were eager to get their hands on the allotted land and were not willing to wait the full twenty-five years. In response, in 1906 Congress passed the Burke Act to allow for competency hearings whereby tribal members who were deemed to be competent would immediately receive a fee patent for their property.[4] During this same session, Congress passed a specific provision applicable to the Oneida reservation. That provision provided primarily for the issuance of fee patents to certain named individuals but also authorized the secretary of the interior in his discretion to issue fee patents to any Indian on the Oneida reservation and provided that "the issuance of such patent shall operate as a removal of all restrictions as to the sale, taxation and alienation of the lands so patented."[5] Most of this newly fee patented land quickly fell out of tribal member ownership. Within a single generation, tribal members lost title to 90 percent of the land through land sales, mortgage foreclosures, and tax foreclosures.[6] During this time, the Wisconsin legislature also created two towns on the reservation: the Town of Hobart and the Town of Oneida. The Town of Hobart would later become the Village of Hobart.

Prior to allotment, and despite colonization, removal, and assimilation, the Oneida people maintained our agricultural lifestyle, and neighbors would gather to help one another during the planting season all the way through harvest. In the 1930s and 1940s, the Oneida people shared stories as part of Franklin Roosevelt's New Deal program the Works Progress Administration. This collection is full of stories about the impacts of allotment and the trauma that ensues when a communal, agricultural people have lost almost all of their land within a single generation and the churches and federal government advance policies of private land ownership and individualism.[7] These concepts were foreign to our people and ran counter to our original teachings. This was more than a rapid loss of land; it was a rapid loss of a way of life. The Oneida people today still feel the remnants of that policy. Reacquiring the land will not, by itself, heal our community. However, it is one significant step in that direction.

In 1934 Congress changed its policy toward tribes and passed the Indian Reorganization Act (IRA).[8] The goals of this Act were to stop the alienation of tribal lands, to restore the management of tribal affairs to tribal governments, and to put in place a mechanism for tribes to rebuild their land bases, which had been devastated by the previous allotment policies. Pursuant to this Act, the Nation adopted a new constitution and began working with the federal government to reacquire ownership of land lost through the allotment process and to have that land placed back into trust status.[9] This process is known as the fee-to-trust process. As noted, the Oneida people lost ownership of 90 percent of the land on the reservation in one generation; it has taken 90 years to reacquire just over 40 percent of that land, and only half of that land has been transferred back into trust status.

Development of Reservation Land

In 1973 the Oneida Nation developed a Comprehensive Plan for the Oneida reservation.[10] The plan focused on potential uses of land owned by the Nation currently at the time, 2,516 acres, less than 4 percent of the land on the reservation.[11] This number does not include land owned by individual tribal members in fee or in trust status as there was not an established system to track such information. The plan focused on housing, health, education, and economic development efforts.

The following year, the Village[12] developed a comprehensive plan that included a future 170-acre industrial park in the southeast part of the reservation in an agricultural area.[13] Ten years later, the Village designated 490 acres for the industrial park. It wasn't until 1995 that the Village began to undertake efforts to implement the plan and it eventually expended approximately $5 million to provide sewer, water, gas, roads, and other improvements to the area. In 2001, the Village obtained a government bond to extend an existing road, O'Hare Boulevard, to serve as the main road running through the proposed industrial park. On June 26, 2001, the Village Board adopted an order laying out the road extension, authorizing acquisition of a road right-of-way, and levying special assessments. The Village's plans did not align with the Nation's plans for this area or for the reservation as a whole.[14]

The only way to ensure that the Nation could control development in the proposed industrial park was to acquire the property. In 2000 the Nation acquired ninety-eight acres in the proposed industrial park.[15] In 2001, on the same day the Village Board took action to extend O'Hare Boulevard through the proposed industrial park, the Nation acquired another 274 acres. That acquisition resulted in Nation owning over 75 percent of the proposed 490 acre site. Soon after acquisition, the Nation informed the Village it objected to the extension of O'Hare Boulevard over tribal property including installation of water and sewer lines, curb and gutter, and electrical lines along the road extension. This property became known as the O'Hare Boulevard property. When the Village informed the Nation it was going to continue with the project, the Nation informed the Village that state condemnation laws could not be utilized against land owned by a tribal government. The Village's response was to file a lawsuit in state court.

While the Village's lawsuit was pending, the Nation saw an opportunity to protect an environmentally sensitive area in the northern part of the reservation from development. In 2006 the Nation purchased a seventeen-acre parcel and obtained a right of first refusal and conservation easement over land adjoining that parcel.[16] This property was located near a road called Forest Road and was later referred to as the Forest Road property. The Village later informed the Nation of its plans to condemn this property for water and sewer lines.

THE FEDERAL CONDEMNATION CASE

The Village filed suit in the circuit court for Brown County against tribal elected officials and tribal employees and sought a declaration that tribal fee land was subject to the Village's condemnation authority. The Village claimed that these tribal officials had acted outside the scope of their authority by denying that tribal fee land was subject to state condemnation procedures. The Nation argued that the tribal officials were immune from suit and that the state court lacked jurisdiction over the controversy.

After the state court declined to dismiss the Village's lawsuit against tribal officials, the Nation sued the Village in federal court in 2006 seeking declaratory and injunctive relief prohibiting the Village from condemning the O'Hare Boulevard and Forest Road properties. The state court proceedings were stayed, the Village filed counterclaims against the Nation in the federal lawsuit, and the Nation and the Village eventually filed cross-motions for summary judgment. The Nation asked the court to declare that fee land within the reservation was exempt from condemnation and the imposition of special assessments and sought return of the assessments previously paid. The Village sought a declaration that tribal fee land was subject to the Village's condemnation authority and special assessments, as well as a monetary judgment in the amount of the unpaid assessments. The land at issue had previously been allotted under the General Allotment Act, had fallen out of tribal member ownership, had been reacquired by the Nation, and had not yet gone through the process to be placed into trust status.

The Nation relied on two main arguments in the federal court proceedings. First, the Nation contended that the Indian Reorganization Act prohibits the Village from condemning the Nation's fee property without the Nation's consent.[17] Second, the Nation contended that the Indian Nonintercourse Act prohibits the Village from condemning the Nation's fee property without congressional consent.[18] However, before getting into those laws, it is important to revisit the historic allotment acts and the legal implications for tribal land today.

Alienability and
In Rem Jurisdiction over Land

Decisions of the Supreme Court of the United States (SCOTUS) set the framework for how land previously lost through allotment and reacquired by tribes and tribal members is to be treated. In *County of Yakima v. Confederated Tribes and Bands of the Yakima Nation*, SCOTUS considered whether ad valorem property taxes (real estate taxes based on the value of the land) and excise taxes (taxes imposed on the transfer of title to land, similar to a sales tax) could be assessed against tribally owned on-reservation fee land that had previously been allotted.[19] The Yakima Nation asserted the taxes were invalid and refused to pay them. The Court relied on its prior decision in *Goudy v. Meath*, in which it found that land which is alienable is also taxable.[20] Applying this principle, the Court found that the General Allotment Act expressly allowed for the alienation and taxation of allotted land and that the Yakima Nation's purchase of the land did not change this result. The Court reached a different conclusion regarding the excise tax. While the ad valorem tax was a permissible burden on the land, the excise tax was a burden on the people involved in the sales transaction and was invalid.

SCOTUS reasoned that while states have the power to tax land, "the excise tax remains a tax upon the Indian's activity of selling the land, and thus is void, whatever means may be devised for its collection."[21] A few years later, in *Cass County v. Leech Lake Band of Chippewa Indians*, SCOTUS again considered the taxability of land previously allotted under a different allotment act (the Nelson Act), subsequently acquired by nonmembers and then reacquired by the Leech Lake Band. The Court relied on the same reasoning and found the repurchased land was subject to taxation.[22] SCOTUS further explained that the fee-to-trust provisions of the IRA serve as a mechanism to restore the tax-exempt status of reservation land.

In *Gobin v. Snohomish County*, the United States Court of Appeals for the Ninth Circuit considered whether a local government could regulate the use of previously allotted land acquired in fee status by a tribal member on her reservation.[23] Gobin wanted to subdivide her land for a residential development. She obtained tribal permits for her project under the tribe's zoning ordinance. The county asserted that she was also required to comply with its zoning laws and raised concerns about the protection of endangered species, the regulation of county roads, and uniformity in the application of zoning codes. The county also argued that the Supreme Court had already determined in *Yakima* and *Cass County* that Congress had granted local governments in rem jurisdiction over lands that were alienable. The Court of Appeals rejected the county's arguments and determined the county's zoning laws impermissibly burdened Gobin's use of the land and activities and transactions involving the land.

> Congress's decision to make Indian fee lands freely alienable is not an express authorization or otherwise an "unmistakably clear" indication that the County may enforce its in rem land use regulations over those lands. Unlike the inextricably linked concepts of (forced) alienation and taxation found in County of Yakima, alienation and plenary in rem land use regulation are entirely unrelated. Thus, we hold that the right of Indians to alienate their lands freely does not provide the County with a concomitant right to exert in rem land use regulation over those lands.[24]

This holding is consistent with that in *Alaska v. Native Village of Venetie*, in which SCOTUS noted that "generally speaking, primary jurisdiction over land that is Indian country rests with the Federal Government and the Indian tribe inhabiting it, and not with the States."[25]

In short, these SCOTUS decisions determined that local governments could assess property taxes on reservation tribal fee land based on the value of the land but not on transactions involving land such as excise taxes. The reasoning is that Congress never granted states or local governments this latter authority. For example, if a tribal citizen owns land on the reservation, that person is responsible for paying annual property taxes based on the value of the land. However, if a tribal citizen owns his or her own land on the reservation and sells that land to another tribal citizen, the local government cannot impose a tax on the sale. Similarly, the Court of Appeals in *Gobin* took these cases to find that Congress had never granted states or local governments the ability to zone tribal citizen fee land on the reservation. The Nation argued that if the Village lacked the authority to do anything except impose real estate taxes, it surely lacked the authority to condemn Nation-owned land on the reservation.

The Impact of the Indian Reorganization Act

One argument the Nation advanced in its federal lawsuit against the Village was that the Indian Reorganization Act protected the land from being taken without the Nation's consent. The intent of the Indian Reorganization Act was, in part, to stop the loss of tribal land. Section 16 of the IRA grants Indian tribes the right to organize for their common welfare and to adopt constitutions and bylaws by majority vote of the adult tribal members. Pursuant to the IRA, each tribe organized under an IRA constitution is expressly vested with certain enumerated rights and powers. One such power relates to the protection of tribal lands and assets. The IRA provides that an IRA constitution "shall also vest in such tribe or its tribal council the following rights and powers: . . . to prevent the sale, disposition, lease, or encumbrance of tribal lands, interests in lands, or other tribal assets without consent of the tribe."[26] In accordance with this language, the Oneida Nation adopted an IRA constitution that includes a provision authorizing the Nation's government to "veto any sale, disposition, lease or encumbrance of tribal lands, interests in lands, or other tribal assets of the tribe."[27]

Congress expressly recognized that the language of Section 476(e) prevented the nonconsensual condemnation of tribal land when it passed a statute in 1948 to establish a general procedure for the secretary of the interior to grant rights-of-way across Indian land.[28] Section 2 of the 1948 Act provides that "no grant of a right-of-way over and across any lands belonging to a tribe organized under the Act of June 18, 1934 [i.e., the IRA] . . . shall be made without the consent of the proper tribal officials."[29]

Only one court had previously addressed the scope of the Section 476(e) veto authority. In *In re 1981, 1982, 1984 and 1985 Delinquent Property Taxes Owed to the City of Nome, Alaska*, the Alaska Supreme Court recognized that no prior case had directly considered the question whether the IRA veto provision applies to state action.[30] The City in that case argued that the provisions of the IRA intended to protect tribes from decisions by the Department of the Interior disposing of tribal lands and assets without the tribe's consent. The court disagreed and held that the IRA veto authority protects fee simple lands held by an IRA tribe against a state's attempt to foreclose upon the lands. The court explained, "It intended to stop erosion of the tribal land base in whatever form that erosion took."[31]

In deciding whether the Village possessed authority to condemn the Nation's fee land, the federal district court considered the federal protections on land reacquired by the Nation. Despite the plain language of the IRA and existing case law, the district court determined that acquisition of land by the Nation did not trigger federal protections. In doing so, the court explained the purpose of Section 16 was twofold. First, it prevented the federal government from disposing of tribal assets without consultation, not local governments. Second, it prevented government bureaucrats from abusing tribal resources. The court explained, "it was not to provide tribes with an alternative means of resurrecting the exemption from state laws their reacquired lands had previously enjoyed."[32] The court further explained that the IRA did not overturn the allotment acts or reinstate restrictions on taxation and alienation that the allotment acts removed.

The Indian Nonintercourse Act

Another argument the Nation advanced was that the Indian Nonintercourse Act (INA) protected the land from alienation without congressional consent. In 1790 Congress passed the INA to control the disposition of Indian lands. The INA states, in part: "That no sale of lands made by any Indians, or any nation or tribe of Indians within the United States, shall be valid to any person or persons, or to any state, whether having the right of preemption to such lands or not, unless the same be made and duly executed at some public treaty, held under the authority of the United States."[33] The INA "was enacted after more than 150 years of conflict between the colonies and the crown, and later the states and the federal government, over control of Indian affairs."[34]

Shortly after its passage, President George Washington explained the purpose of the INA to the Seneca Indians: "Here, then, is the security for the remainder of your lands. No State, nor person, can purchase your lands, unless at some public treaty, held under the authority of the United States. The General Government will never consent to your being defrauded, but it will protect you in all your just rights."[35]

Congress amended the INA a number of times over the years. In its current form, the INA is more expansive than the provision enacted in 1790, except that it no longer protects lands owned by individual Indians. It states in part: "No purchase, grant, lease, or other conveyance of lands, or of any title or claim thereto, from any Indian nation or tribe of Indians, shall be of any validity in law or equity, unless the same be made by treaty or convention entered into pursuant to the Constitution."[36] The INA applies broadly to any "purchase, grant, lease or other conveyance of lands, or any title or claim thereto, from any Indian nation or tribe of Indians."[37] By its plain terms, the INA does not distinguish between lands held in fee by a tribe and lands held in trust for the tribe by the United States, and it does not distinguish among lands on the basis of how or when a tribe acquired the lands.

The Indian Nonintercourse Act was tested in a line of land claims cases starting with *County of Oneida v. Oneida Indian Nation of N.Y. (Oneida II)*.[38] In that case, SCOTUS considered the validity of treaties entered into by the Oneida and the State of New York after passage of the INA. Congress did not approve these treaties. SCOTUS held that the treaties were invalid as they violated federal law and remanded the issue back to the lower courts to determine what damages the counties in New York owed to the Oneidas.[39] The key finding here is that the transfer of land was invalid.

On the basis of the holding in *Oneida II*, the Oneida Indian Nation (OIN) in New York argued that land it had reacquired in the land claim area was exempt from taxation. In *City of Sherrill v. Oneida Indian Nation of New York*, OIN asserted it had reunified aboriginal title and fee title and argued that the City's property taxes were invalid because Congress had never consented to taxation of the land.[40] SCOTUS did not agree and held that a tribe cannot unilaterally reinstate federal protection of its reservation lands simply by making open-market purchases from current titleholders. The Court went on to state that if OIN wanted to restore the tax exempt status of the land, the Indian Reorganization Act provided a mechanism for it to do so. Within the decision, SCOTUS ignored the Oneida people's historic and continuous attempts to invalidate the illegal treaties and to seek remedies through the federal government. Instead, it faulted the OIN for waiting too long to raise the issue. In so ignoring past efforts, SCOTUS offered its infamous proclamation that the law prevented the OIN from "rekindling embers of sovereignty that long ago grew cold."[41]

After SCOTUS determined the land was taxable, the next question that arose was whether a local government could foreclose on tribal property for failure to pay taxes assessed against the property. Courts have since held that the seizure of tribally owned fee lands through foreclosure of property tax liens is prohibited by the INA.[42] In *Oneida Indian Nation v. Madison County*, the United States District Court for the District of New York explained: "The seizing of land owned by a sovereign nation strikes directly at the very heart of that nation's sovereignty. In the face of Federal and State laws and the solemn treaty obligations of the United States, permitting the seizure of lands from a sovereign nation should require, at the very least, a specific Act of Congress."[43] The most recent decision in this line of cases came down in October 2020, when the United States Court of Appeals for the Second Circuit decided *Cayuga Indian Nation v. Seneca County*.[44] In that case, the Second Circuit declined to allow the county to foreclose on tribal property for failure to pay taxes. Seneca County is currently seeking review of this decision by SCOTUS.

District Court's Consideration of the Indian Nonintercourse Act and Sherill

Back to the case at hand. In the Oneida Nation's federal lawsuit against the Village, the Nation argued that the INA prohibits condemnation of on-reservation tribal land regardless of how the land was acquired, but the district court did not agree. Instead, the district court determined that the General Allotment Act required congressional consent to alienate the land and distinguished the OIN cases because OIN's land had not been allotted under the GAA. The district court also disagreed with the holding of those cases that foreclosure is not an available remedy for a local government to collect property taxes assessed against tribal fee land. The district court instead commented that, "unless a state or local government is able to foreclose on Indian property for nonpayment of taxes, the authority to tax such property is meaningless."[45] The district court stated its rationale as follows:

> I conclude, contrary to the district court in the *Oneida Indian Nation* cases on remand from *Sherill*, that implicit in the Court's holding that Indian fee lands are subject to ad valorem property taxes is the further holding that such lands can be forcibly sold for nonpayment of such taxes. And, of course, if Indian lands are not exempt from forced alienation for nonpayment of state or local property taxes, it also follows that they are not exempt from the Village's power to condemn such land for a public highway and, further, to assess such property for the cost of improvements that specially benefit the property.[46]

CLOSING OBSERVATIONS

The Village has yet to extend O'Hare Boulevard across the Nation's property, and the Nation still owns 372 acres of the 490-acre proposed industrial park, effectively stopping development of the majority of the area. For the Forest Road property, the Village obtained an easement from the Nation and ran water and sewer lines through Nation's property to access a 600-acre residential and commercial development in the northern part of the reservation called Centennial Centre.[47]

While we were briefing this litigation, I prepared an affidavit that covered a variety of topics, including my personal family history, the tribal easement process, acquisition of O'Hare Boulevard and Forest Road properties, an analysis of the fee and trust patents issued pursuant to allotment, pending fee-to-trust applications for the O'Hare and Forest Road properties, real estate taxes, the terminated service agreement between the Nation and the Village, and the first time Elaine Willman came to the reservation.[48] The first segment of my affidavit is particularly relevant to this story. It demonstrates the enduring connection between the Oneida people and our land base. I pulled a single line in my family tree to illustrate that connection as well as our service to the military. The last paragraph in this section also ties my husband's family directly to the O'Hare Boulevard property. The following is an excerpt from my affidavit:

2. I am an enrolled member of the Tribe. I reside on the Oneida Indian Reservation (the "Reservation") and within the boundaries of the Village of Hobart. . . . Except for an approximately five-year period of time during which I attended the University of Wisconsin–Madison, I have lived on the Reservation or in the immediate vicinity of the Reservation for my entire life.

3. I am personally familiar with my family history, both through reading historical materials and discussions with family members and relatives. My maternal great-great-great-great-grandfather was Cornelius Doxtator. He was born in 1817 on the Oneida Reservation in New York, and was named after a relative of the same name who headed the Pagan Party and

who died in the Battle of Chippewa fighting on the American side during the War of 1812. Both men were descendants of Honyerry and Hanyost Dockstader (Doxtator), who were distinguished officers in General Washington's Patriot Army in the American Revolution. Like his namesake and forefathers, Cornelius Doxtator served in the military. During the Civil War, he was a private in the F Company, Fourteenth Wisconsin Voluntary Infantry.

Cornelius Doxtator and his family moved to the Wisconsin Territory in the 1820s, and he lived the majority of his life on the Reservation. As an educated man who was able to read, write and speak English, he also served as an Oneida delegate and official representative to Albany, NY, Madison, WI, and Washington, D.C. On at least one occasion, he appeared before the Indian Department in Washington, D.C., to oppose imposition of an elected form of government as a replacement for the hereditary chieftainship system. He died in 1911 on the Reservation, and is buried at the Episcopal cemetery at the Church of the Holy Apostles on the Reservation.

4. Two of Cornelius Doxtator's sons, Paul Doxtator and my maternal great-great-great grandfather, Henry "Duke" Doxtator, were vocal critics of the patenting of allotted Reservation lands. They feared that the loss of the tribal land base would create beggars of tribal members. Henry "Duke" Doxtator was born in 1853 on the Reservation, and lived on the Reservation for his entire life. He received an allotment of 89.85 acres. He died in 1944 and is buried at the Oneida United Methodist Church on the Reservation.

5. Henry "Duke" Doxtator's son, my maternal great-great grandfather, was Chauncey Doxtator. He was born in 1884 on the Reservation, and lived his entire life on the Reservation. He received an allotment of 26 acres. He spoke out against the patenting of trust allotments and called for unity among the Oneida people in order to bring about a change in policy and a change in BIA leadership. He died in 1951 and is buried at the Oneida United Methodist Church on the Reservation.

6. Chauncey Doxtator's daughter, my maternal great grandmother, was Pauline King nee Doxtator. She was born in 1911 on the Reservation. At the age of four, she was sent to Flandreau Indian School in South

Dakota. She ran away from the boarding school and returned to the Reservation when she was 13 or 14 years old. She lived the majority of her adult life in the City of Green Bay, Wisconsin. Oneida was her first language, and I recall as a child hearing her speak Oneida. She died in 1985 and is buried at Episcopal cemetery at the Church of the Holy Apostles on the Reservation.

7. Pauline King's son, my maternal grandfather, is Michael King. He was born in 1940 on the Reservation. He has lived the majority of his adult life in the City of Green Bay, Wisconsin. He currently resides on the Reservation. My mother, Michele King, was born in . . . the City of Green Bay, Wisconsin. She has lived on or near the Reservation for her entire life, and is employed as the manager of the Tribe's retail division.

8. I am married to Stephen Webster, who is also an enrolled member of the Tribe. I am personally familiar with aspects of his family history. His great-great-great grandfather was Moses Webster, who was one of the original allottees who received a fee patent for allotted land within what now comprises the Tribe's O'Hare Boulevard Property.

My grandfather has since passed on and is also buried on the Oneida reservation in the Oneida Nation Cemetery. I often wonder what my ancestors would think of these lawsuits, especially this lawsuit. The Oneida people have a history of constantly trying to protect our land from encroachments, greedy land speculators, and unscrupulous land deals. It seems quite unjust that the Court decided we could not protect the land we had to repurchase on our own reservation.

Notes

1. R. M. Webster, "This Land Can Sustain Us: Cooperative Land Use Planning on the Oneida Reservation," *Planning Theory and Practice* 17, no. 1 (2016): 9–34. doi: 10.1080/14649357.2015.1135250.

2. Oneida Tribe v. Hobart, 542 F.Supp.2d 908, 921 (E.D. Wis. 2008).

3. General Allotment Act, 25 U.S.C. ch. 9 §331 et seq. (1887). See chap. 3 for a more complete discussion about the allotment acts.

4. Burke Act, 34 Stat. 182 (1906).

5. 34 Stat. 325 ch. 3504.

6. A. Locklear, "The Allotment of the Oneida Reservation and Its Legal Ramifications," in J. Campisi and L. M. Hauptman, eds., *The Oneida Indian Experience* (83–93). New York: Syracuse University Press, 1988.

7. R. M. Webster, "The Wisconsin Oneida and the WPA: Stories of Corn, Colonialism and Revitalization," *Ethnohistory* 68, no. 3 (2021).

8. Indian Reorganization Act, 25 U.S.C. ch. 14, subch. V §461 et seq. (1934). See chap. 2 for a more complete discussion about the Indian Reorganization Act.

9. See chap. 9 for a more in-depth discussion about what trust status means and why the Oneida Nation wants to have its land taken into trust status.

10. 701 Comprehensive Planning Program Oneida Indian Reservation (1973).

11. Oneida Reservation Comprehensive Plan (2008), 4–107, accessed March 29, 2021, https://oneida-nsn.gov/dl-file.php?file=2016/02/Comp-Plan-which-includes-Land-Policy-Framework.pdf.

12. Prior to 2002, the Village of Hobart was the Town of Hobart. In 2002, the Town of Hobart incorporated as a village. For consistency in reading, this chapter refers to Hobart as the Village.

13. Tribe's Brief in Support of Motion for Summary Judgment, Oneida Tribe v. Hobart, 542 F.Supp.2d 908.

14. See Oneida Reservation Comprehensive Plan (2005–2025) for current and historical information on tribal planning efforts, accessed March 3, 2021, https://oneida-nsn.gov/dl-file.php?file=2016/02/Comp-Plan-which-includes-Land-Policy-Framework.pdf.

15. Oneida Tribe v. Hobart, 542 F.Supp.2d 908, 913.

16. Oneida Tribe v. Hobart, 542 F.Supp.2d 908, 914. Internal citations omitted.

17. 25 U.S.C. §476 (1934).

18. 25 U.S.C. §177 (1790).

19. 502 U.S. 251 (1991).

20. 203 U.S. 146 (1906).

21. County of Yakima v. Confederated Tribes and Bands of the Yakima Nation, 502 U.S. 251, 269.

22. 524 U.S. 103 (1998).

23. 304 F.3d 909 (9th Cir. 2002). The land at issue in this case was allotted pursuant to the Treaty of Point Elliot, 12 Stat. 927 (January 22, 1855). The legal implications for the treatment of land allotted pursuant to the Treaty of Point Eliot and the General Allotment Act are the same once the land became freely alienable.

24. 304 F.3d at 916.

25. Alaska v. Native Village of Venetie Tribal Gov't, 522 U.S. 520, 527 n. 1, 118 S. Ct. 948, 140 L. Ed. 2d 30 (1998).

26. 25 U.S.C. §476(e). The legislative history also supports the determination that these protections were intended to extend to tribal fee land, the lands most vulnerable to alienation from Indian ownership. See "To Grant to Indians Living under Federal Tutelage the Freedom to Organize for Purposes of Local Self-Government and Economic Enterprise," Hearings on S. 2755 and S. 3645 Before the Senate Comm. on Indian Affairs, 73d Cong. 60–61, 117, 132–34, 148–50, 175, 213, 220 (1934).

27. Oneida Constitution, Article IV, Section 1(c).

28. Act of February 5, 1948, 62 Stat. 17 (codified as amended at 25 U.S.C. §§323–328).

29. 25 U.S.C. §324.

30. 780 P.2d 363 (Alaska 1989).

31. In re 1981, 1982, 1983, 1984 & 1985 Delinquent Property Taxes Owed to the City of Nome, 780 P.2d 363, 367 (Alaska 1989).

32. Oneida Tribe v. Hobart, 542 F.Supp.2d 908, 929.

33. Act of July 22, 1790, ch. 33, §4, 1 Stat. 137.

34. Robert N. Clinton and Margaret Tobey Hotopp, "Judicial Enforcement of the Federal Restraints on Alienation of Indian Land: The Origins of the Eastern Land Claims," *Maine Law Review* 31 (1979): 17, 18.

35. Clinton and Hotopp, "Judicial Enforcement," 37 (quoting from W. Lowrie and M. St. Clair Clarke, eds., *American State Papers: Indian Affairs* (Washington, D.C.: Gales and Seaton, 1832), vol. 1, 142.

36. 25 U.S.C. §177.

37. 25 U.S.C. §177.

38. 470 U. S. 226 (1985). In a prior case, SCOTUS determined that it had jurisdiction over the issue and remanded the case back to the lower courts. Oneida Indian Nation of N. Y. v. County of Oneida, 414 U.S. 661, 664 (1974).

39. The test case was against Oneida County and Madison County and was remanded for a determination of damages owed by the counties for possession of the land for a limited period of time. The lawsuit against the State of New York with respect to the entire reservation was filed on the basis of the result in the test case.

40. 544 U.S. 197 (2005).

41. 544 U.S. 197, 214.

42. Oneida Indian Nation of New York v. Madison County, 605 F.3d 149 (2d Cir. 2010) ("Oneida I"), vacated and remanded sub nom. Madison County v. Oneida Indian Nation of New York, 562 U.S. 42 (2011); Cayuga Indian

Nation of New York v. Seneca County, 761 F.3d 218 (2d Cir. 2014) ("Cayuga I")
(preliminary injunction decision); Cayuga Indian Nation of New York v. Seneca County, No. 19-0032 (2d Cir. 2020).
43. 401 F. Supp. 2d 219 at 232 (N.D.N.Y. 2005).
44. Cayuga Indian Nation v. Seneca County, No. 19-0032 (2d Cir. 2020).
45. Oneida Tribe v. Hobart, 542 F.Supp.2d 908, 921.
46. Oneida Tribe v. Hobart, 542 F.Supp.2d 908, 921.
47. Richard Ryman, "Hobart Plans '100 Percent Walkable' Downtown,"
Green Bay Press Gazette, December 18, 2014, https://www.greenbaypressgazette
.com/story/news/local/2014/12/18/hobart-plans-percent-walkable-downtown/
20605839.
48. See chap. 3 for a discussion on Elaine Willman.

CHAPTER 5

Dispatching the Police

Brown County and Oneida Nation
Intergovernmental Agreement

REBECCA M. WEBSTER

KEY TERMS IN THIS CHAPTER

- Tribal sovereign immunity
- Intergovernmental agreement
- Home rule

Municipal, county, and tribal governments occupy shared spaces within the Oneida reservation. Roughly the eastern half of the reservation overlaps with Brown County. Both the County and the Nation operate police services within that shared space. In 2008, the Oneida Nation and Brown County entered into an intergovernmental agreement to address a variety of mutual governmental service concerns including the County's responsibility to dispatch law enforcement officers to 911 calls. In the intergovernmental agreement, the Nation and the County identified a 1,700-acre area of their shared space that had a significant Oneida tribal member population, including the Oneida Police Department building. In this 1,700-acre area, the County and the Nation agreed it would best serve the community for the County to dispatch Oneida law enforcement officers to 911 calls.

This 1,700-acre area is also located in the Village of Hobart. The Village perceived this as removing authority from the Village to respond to 911 calls and filed suit in Brown County Circuit Court. The court dismissed claims against the Nation on sovereign immunity grounds and later granted summary judgment in favor of the County, rejecting the Village's claims. The Village appealed, and the Wisconsin Court of Appeals affirmed the lower court's decision. The Village asked the Wisconsin Supreme Court to review the decision. The Supreme Court denied the Village's request.

BACKGROUND

History of Intergovernmental Agreements

The Oneida reservation is host to two county governments and five municipal governments. The Oneida reservation also contains various modes of land ownership. The Oneida Nation and individual tribal members own land in fee status (taxable). The United States owns land that it holds in trust for the Nation and individual tribal members (nontaxable). Other governments, nontribal members, and nonprofit organizations also own land on the reservation. All these different types of land ownership are scattered throughout the reservation. This mix of tribal and local governments along with the variety of land ownership requires coordination when determining how the governments provide services to the community.

Most of the governments on the reservation want to provide the most efficient services to the community, and intergovernmental agreements can be a tool for the Nation and local governments to collaborate and streamline their respective services. The Nation began entering into intergovernmental agreements in 1996. Then Governor Tommy Thompson took notice of the Nation's efforts to negotiate these agreements and the positive impact these agreements brought to tribal and local relationships. When the Nation negotiated the 1998 amendment to the Nation's Gaming Compact, the Nation agreed it would "take reasonable action" to enter into intergovernmental agreements with local governments. This 1998 amendment also provided a credit of up to $550,000 for payments made to local governments under the agreements. This meant that the Nation would be able to deduct up to $550,000 from the amount it would otherwise pay to the state as part of the Gaming Compact payment, keeping more money in the local economy. In 2003, the Nation and the State amended the Gaming Compact again and removed the requirement that the Nation take reasonable action to enter into intergovernmental agreements with local governments but increased the credit for payments made to local governments to $1.5 million, thereby keeping even more money in the local economy.

The Nation provides services to tribal members, including health care, elder care, social services, housing, public works, waste and recycling pickup, and education, and it receives credits for these services under the intergovernmental agreements. The Nation also provides services to all residents of the Oneida reservation and receives credits for them. These services include police protection, parks and recreation areas, cultural events, libraries, hunting permits, wetland/woodland/habitat restoration, public transportation and utility services. In making these services available to tribal members and to residents of the reservation, the Nation decreases the cost to other local governments of providing services.

Intergovernmental agreements are also a way for the Nation to coordinate with local governments regarding services they provide that the Nation does not provide. For example, the Town of Oneida has a fire department and first responders whereas the Nation has neither. This means the Town is responsible for providing these services to all community members in the Town. Under state and federal law, the Nation is not bound by state and local fire codes or subject to inspections. However, the Nation recognized that in an emergency, everyone benefits if Town officials are familiar with tribal buildings when they must respond to an emergency. As a result, in its intergovernmental agreement with the Town, the Nation agreed to give the Town annual building access and the ability to conduct drills and to make floor plans available to the Town so the Town can be best prepared to respond in the event of an emergency.

While not all intergovernmental agreements involve a payment from one party to the other, these agreements can provide a way for the Nation to compensate local governments for services provided to tribal trust property while also recognizing the services the Nation provides. Keeping with the Town of Oneida example, the Nation does not pay taxes on tribal trust land; however, the Town still provides government services such as first responders and fire protection to everyone in that part of the reservation. In that agreement, the Nation pays the Town for the services it provides, while recognizing the Nation also provides services to all community members.

One of the benefits to the Nation of intergovernmental agreements is that some of them define the terms under which the local government will not oppose the Nation's applications to have land placed back into trust status and removed from the local tax rolls. Those provisions facilitate the Nation's continued efforts to restore the land base that was devastated through federal policy generations ago. Even though it took less than a generation for the Nation and its members to lose the majority of land ownership on the reservation, it will take many generations to restore the land base. Instead of opposing and further delaying this already slow federal process of restoring trust status to the land, many local governments see the benefits of working cooperatively.

Intergovernmental agreements can also address cooperative land use planning efforts and recognize the limits on municipal civil regulatory authority. These can be important components of an agreement, especially considering the mix of different governments and types of land ownership on the reservation. The Nation has learned through successful and unsuccessful relationships with its neighbors that good governance is enhanced with positive government-to-government relations. The Nation and local governments need a clear understanding of each other's roles, responsibilities, and jurisdiction and need to respect each government's right to exist and exercise its jurisdiction. Some governments seek to change existing federal Indian laws and policies to disestablish tribal governments and Indian reservations. This approach ensures that limited government resources will continue to be directed to litigation.

With an uncertain economic future, it is increasingly important to explore cost-effective ways for our governments to work cooperatively. Intergovernmental agreements between the Nation and surrounding local governments are founded on mutual respect and serve as a pledge that tribal and local governments are committed to maintaining positive government-to-government relationships for the benefit of all community members. The Nation currently has intergovernmental agreements with the City of Green Bay, the Town of Oneida, Outagamie County, and Brown County.

Tribal Enforcement of State Laws

The Oneida Police Department was established in 1985.[1] When the Village filed its lawsuit challenging the dispatch provisions of the intergovernmental agreement, the department employed twenty fully trained and certified law enforcement officers who are authorized to enforce state laws under two different state laws.

The first law allows county sheriffs to deputize tribal law enforcement officers to grant law enforcement and arrest powers anywhere within the reservation boundaries as well as off the reservation throughout the county.[2] The Brown County sheriff has been deputizing Oneida Police Department officers since 2003, and the Outagamie County sheriff has been deputizing Oneida Police Department officers since 2014, and there were earlier dispatch agreements with both sheriffs.

The second law allows a tribal law enforcement officer to enforce state laws anywhere within a tribe's reservation if two conditions are met. First, the tribal law enforcement officer must obtain the same state certifications as state and local law enforcement officers.[3] Second, the tribal government must either accept liability for the acts and omissions of the officer and (1) waive tribal sovereign immunity to allow for suits in state court based upon the acts and omissions of the officer while acting within the scope of his or her employment or (2) obtain liability insurance coverage of not less than $2 million for any occurrence.[4] The tribal government must also provide documentation to the Wisconsin Department of Justice that it has met these requirements.[5]

In 1996 the Oneida Nation adopted Resolution 3-13-96-C, in which it accepted liability for the acts and omissions of its officers and waived its sovereign immunity to allow enforcement of this liability in state court. Pursuant to section 195.92(3m)(b), the Wisconsin Department of

Justice determined that Resolution 3-13-96-C would "reasonably allow" for enforcement of the Nation's liability and posted notice on its law enforcement information network. Since that time, the Oneida Police Department, the Wisconsin Law Enforcement Standards Board, the Brown County District Attorney's Office, the Outagamie County District Attorney's Office, and other law enforcement agencies have relied upon the Wisconsin Department of Justice's determination under section 165.92(3)(6)(2) that Resolution 3-13-96-C would "reasonably allow" for enforcement of the Tribe's liability for the acts of its officers.[6]

While the Village's lawsuit was pending, the Oneida Nation Business Committee rescinded the 1996 resolution and replaced it with an updated version. The updated tribal resolution included the relevant language of sections 165.92(3)(a) and (3)(b)(l) pertaining to the Tribe's liability for the acts of its law enforcement officers and a waiver of the Tribe's sovereign immunity to permit enforcement of that liability. The resolution recognized the continued commitment of the Nation with respect to its liability for the acts of its law enforcement officers. In part, the resolution provided that the "Oneida Tribe continues to accept liability for all acts of each Oneida Police Department law enforcement officer while acting within the scope of his or her employment, and the Oneida Business Committee hereby waives the Oneida Tribe's sovereign immunity to the extent necessary to allow the enforcement in the courts of the State of Wisconsin of this liability in accordance with section 165.92(3) (a) of the Wisconsin Statutes."[7]

Village Establishment of Law Enforcement

In 2001 the Village partnered with a neighboring municipal government, the Town of Lawrence, to form a police department.[8] After the formation of this new joint police department, the Brown County dispatch began to dispatch Hobart/Lawrence police officers to 911 calls made within the portion of the reservation occupied by the Village, including calls originating from properties owned by the Nation and tribal members. This was a concern for the Nation because at the time, the Village police operated on only a part-time basis and had limited resources and coverage and, at times, slow response times.[9]

*Intergovernmental Agreement between the
Nation and Brown County*

Elected officials from the Oneida Nation and Brown County signed the intergovernmental agreement on May 29, 2008. This agreement covers a wide variety of topics, including payment to the County for services it provides to the Nation's trust land, the County's agreement not to oppose the Nation's applications to have land placed into trust, dispatch of law enforcement officers, planning for emergency services, and the sharing of information.

The relevant portion of the intergovernmental agreement in this instance centers on the dispatching of Oneida police officers to a 1,700-acre area commonly referred to as "downtown Oneida." This area is inhabited primarily by tribal members and is the location of tribal businesses and governmental offices, including the Oneida Nation Police Department. Paragraph 3 of the intergovernmental agreement, titled Law Enforcement, provided:

a. The Tribe shall provide primary police service protection for those geographic areas designated in Attachment A. The parties agree to update Attachment A as circumstances may warrant.
b. The Tribe shall call for mutual aid in the form of back-up/secondary assistance for police, ambulance, emergency medical or rescue services when needed.
c. The County shall provide mutual aid in the form of back-up/secondary assistance for police services and protection to persons and property when requested by the tribe.
d. When requested by the County, the Tribe shall provide mutual aid in the form of secondary/back-up assistance for police, ambulance, emergency medical or rescue services, within the limitations of services provided by the Tribe.

This paragraph ensured that 911 calls emerging from "downtown Oneida" would have an Oneida Police Department officer dispatched to the scene. Furthermore, these provisions are in line with the state statutes promoting intergovernmental cooperation between Wisconsin municipalities and Indian tribes, including those specifically permitting county–tribal law enforcement agreements.[10]

HOBART VILLAGE'S CHALLENGE TO THE INTERGOVERNMENTAL AGREEMENT

The 1,700 acres known as "downtown Oneida" are also located within the Village of Hobart. When the village officials learned of the provisions in the intergovernmental agreement relating to the law enforcement dispatch, they perceived it as an infringement on the Village's supposed "exclusive authority over the provision of law enforcement services within its jurisdiction."[11] The Village sued both the County and the Nation in Brown County Circuit Court, challenging the validity of the dispatch provisions.

A Challenge to the Legitimacy of the Oneida Police Department

The Village claimed the Oneida Police Department and its law enforcement officers did not possess any policing authority for a variety of reasons, which the courts summarily rejected. Among its claims, the Village brought up a number of unsubstantiated "what if" scenarios, including unsubstantiated speculation the Nation might not purchase an insurance policy, that the tribal resolution and insurance policy might not cover every conceivable claim for damages, that the tribal resolution and insurance policy might not allow for declaratory and injunctive relief, or that the Nation might nonetheless interpose the defense of sovereign immunity.

The Village also claimed that the Nation's sovereign immunity would prevent declaratory or injunctive relief for civil rights violations by individual Oneida Nation law enforcement officers. The Village's claims were without merit and were unsupported by existing case law. Tribal sovereign immunity does not preclude declaratory or injunctive relief against tribal officials or officers who are acting in violation of federal law.[12] This is exactly the same relief that is available against state officials or officers who are acting in violation of federal law.

The Village presented a series of convoluted arguments in an attempt to show that the Nation's resolution accepting liability for the acts and omissions of its officers was somehow deficient and that the Oneida Police Department therefore lacked authority to enforce state law. All of these arguments failed to take into account the state law that authorizes County sheriffs to deputize tribal law enforcement officers to enforce state law and the Brown County sheriff's long-standing deputization of Oneida Police Department officers pursuant to that law.

The Village's Claim of Exclusive Authority to Dispatch Police Officers

The Village also argued that it has exclusive authority over law enforcement within its boundaries under Wisconsin's "home rule" constitutional provisions and statutes. In general, the "home rule" provisions of the Wisconsin Constitution and statutes outline a process whereby cities and villages are permitted to govern themselves with respect to local matters without the state legislature interfering or being involved.[13] However, this argument was misplaced with respect to the County's ability to dispatch law enforcement officers from different jurisdictions. Either the Village possesses "exclusive authority" and every provision of the Wisconsin Constitution and statutes recognizing or granting concurrent law enforcement authority to another governmental entity is invalid, or the Village does not possess such "exclusive authority." The Village's argument essentially asked the court to rule that the enforcement of state laws is solely a matter of local concern, although the laws themselves are enacted by the state legislature and enforced by numerous agencies, including the state police, county sheriffs, district attorneys for the counties, and the circuit courts for the counties. The court rightfully rejected this absurd claim.

Clarification Amendment to the Intergovernmental Agreement

During the initial briefing process before the court, the County and the Nation decided to amend the portion of the intergovernmental agreement that addresses law enforcement. The September 18, 2008, amendments served two main purposes: first, to add references to the existing authority of Oneida Police Department officers under Wisconsin law and, second, to emphasize that the intergovernmental agreement did not take any authority away from any other jurisdiction. Both of these revisions addressed mischaracterizations made by the Village regarding the dispatch provisions. The relevant provisions of the new language of the amendment are as follows:

a. Law enforcement officers of the Oneida Police Department are authorized to enforce state law within the boundaries of the Oneida Reservation pursuant to section 165.92 of the Wisconsin Statutes, and are also deputized by the Sheriff of Brown County to enforce state law and keep the peace within the County pursuant to section 59.26(5) of the Wisconsin Statutes. The Oneida Business Committee, as the governing body of the Tribe, has adopted a Resolution which (1) accepts liability for the acts of Oneida Police Department law enforcement officers while acting in the scope of their employment, and (2) waives the Tribe's sovereign immunity to allow enforcement of this liability in the courts of the State of Wisconsin. . . .

f. Nothing in this Agreement is intended to divest any law enforcement agency of jurisdiction or authority to enforce state law.

Encouragement for Coordination of Law Enforcement

The trial court dismissed the Nation as a party on the basis of sovereign immunity grounds and awarded the Nation statutory attorney's fees. The court later granted summary judgment in favor of the County. The Village asked the court to reconsider its decision, claiming the Nation was not a public agency eligible to receive 911 calls under state law. The court denied the Village's motion for reconsideration. The Village appealed to the Wisconsin Court of Appeals and that court affirmed the trial court's decision. The Village then asked the Wisconsin Supreme Court to review the decision. The Supreme Court denied the Village's request.

In its decision, the Wisconsin Court of Appeals commented on the common-sense rationale and legislative intent behind encouraging cooperation among county and tribal law enforcement. The court explained:

Further, the statutes permitting county-tribal law enforcement programs provide strong evidence that the County may designate the tribal police department as the primary responder to 911 calls within the service area. Any county with all or part of a federally recognized Indian reservation within its boundaries may agree with an Indian tribe to establish a cooperative county-tribal law enforcement program.[14] These statutes permit a county and a tribe to agree on a wide range of matters, including the types of law enforcement services to be performed on the reservation, the identity of the service provider, and the identity of the person exercising supervision and control over the program's law enforcement officers.[15] These statutes suggest that the legislature sought to encourage law enforcement coordination between counties and tribes.[16]

This segment of the decision reinforced the cooperative intergovernmental relationships the Nation and County worked to build through the intergovernmental agreement.

CLOSING OBSERVATIONS

The negotiation of the intergovernmental agreement between the Oneida Nation and Brown County was the first that I participated in as a member of the negotiation team. We met with the County for about a year to work out the terms. During that year Nation staff gained a better understanding of County government roles and functions and vice versa. It was a reciprocal process of learning and educating. Over that year, we built on existing positive working relationships at the various levels of government.

After executing the intergovernmental agreement with the County, the Nation began to negotiate a new Intergovernmental agreement with the City of Green Bay. That was a similar learning process for everyone involved. One difference in governing authority between the County and City was the level of government involvement with land use regulatory issues. The City was more involved in these issues. Like the entirety of the Oneida reservation, in areas where the City and the Oneida reservation overlap, there was a mix of land ownership. If a nontribal citizen had a concern over a neighboring property owned by the Nation, that individual likely brought those issues to the attention of City employees. Part of our discussions with the City during these intergovernmental agreement negotiations involved how to resolve these types of issues. In that intergovernmental agreement, we included a provision in which the City recognized that it has limited authority over tribal citizens and the Nation and land owned by them. The intergovernmental agreement also included a process to address complaints brought by City residents. The result was a paragraph titled "Peace and Safety." This paragraph recognized that City ordinances that addressed zoning, building, nuisance, and land use regulations did not apply to the Nation, tribal citizens, or individuals leasing Nation-owned land.

This Peace and Safety provision in the intergovernmental agreement with the City led tribal officials and staff to approach Brown County about including a similar provision in the tribe's intergovernmental agreement with the County. The result was a third amendment to the intergovernmental agreement and the addition of a paragraph titled "Health and Safety." The paragraph mirrored what was in the City intergovernmental agreement with the inclusion of County codes concerning health inspections. These provisions in the City and County intergovernmental agreements were significant because they clarified where City and County jurisdiction over tribal members and tribal land stopped and where the City and County would not interfere with the Nation's exercise of its own jurisdiction. This level of government-to-government cooperation and mutual respect allowed the Nation and local governments to work on issues of mutual concern within their shared spaces.

In the months and years that followed, I sat on the negotiation team for a number of other intergovernmental agreements. Eventually, we had renewed agreements with Outagamie County, Brown County, the Town of Oneida, the City of Green Bay, and the Village of Ashwaubenon. We did not enter into an agreement with the Village of Pittsfield or a new agreement with the Village of Hobart. The Village of Pittsfield and the Oneida reservation overlap in the northernmost corner of the reservation, an area of 196 acres, or roughly 1 percent of the Oneida reservation. The reasoning behind the Nation's inability to secure a renewed agreement with the Village of Hobart should be evident from the contents of this book.

Notes

1. Village of Hobart v. Brown County, 336 Wis.2d 474, 801 N.W.2d 348 (Wis. App. 2011).

2. Wis. Stat. Sec. 59.26(5).

3. Wis. Stat. Sec. 165.92(2)(a).

4. Wis. Stat. Sec. 165.92(3m)(a)(1); Wis. Stat. Sec. 165.92(3m)(a)(2).

5. Wis. Stat. Sec. 165.92(3m)(b).

6. Oneida Nation Business Committee Resolution BC-3-13-96-C.

7. Oneida Nation Business Committee Resolution BC-09-03-08-A.

8. Village of Hobart v. Brown County, 336 Wis.2d 474, 801 N.W.2d 348 (Wis. App. 2011).

9. Brief of Oneida Tribe of Indians of Wisconsin in Opposition to Village of Hobart's Motion for Summary Judgment, filed September 5, 2008.

10. See Wis. Stat. Sec. 165.90.

11. Village of Hobart v. Brown County, 336 Wis.2d 474, 801 N.W.2d 348 (Wis. App. 2011).

12. Santa Clara Pueblo v. Martinez, 436 U.S. 49, 59 (1978) (citing Ex Parte Young, 209 U.S. 123 (1908)).

13. See Wis. Const., Art. XI, sec. 3 (home rule amendments); Wis Stat. 61.34(1) (home rule for Villages).

14. See WIS. STAT. §§59.54(12), 165.90.

15. See §61.65(1)(a)WIS. STAT. §165.90(2)(d),(e).

16. Village of Hobart v. Brown County, 336 Wis.2d 474, 801 N.W.2d 348 (Wis. App. 2011).

CHAPTER 6

ᘉᘉ

Overcoming Restrictive Covenants to Reacquire Reservation Land

REBECCA M. WEBSTER

KEY TERMS IN THIS CHAPTER

- Fee-to-trust
- Zoning jurisdiction
- Tribal sovereign immunity
- Restrictive covenants

The Oneida Nation has a long history of trying to reacquire land within the Oneida reservation boundaries and have that land taken into trust status. Having land taken into trust status helps restore the status of land within our reservation to what it was before federal policy tried to break up our tribal landholdings.[1] While we are rebuilding our land base, our reacquisition has created a checkerboard pattern of ownership. This checkerboard pattern is a constant reminder that we came close to losing ownership of all the land on our reservation. When a hunter exercises treaty rights on tribal land and the deer runs onto a nontribal member's land, that hunter needs permission to retrieve the deer, which is often denied. While people would be quick to point out this happens off the reservation as well, consider the hopscotch of relatively small areas Nation citizens have to hunt on within our reservation boundaries.

Conversely, the Village of Hobart has a history of trying to prevent the Nation from acquiring land and from having land placed into trust status because the Village perceives it as a threat to its tax base and its regulatory authority.[2] One step the Village has taken to prevent the fee-to-trust process is the placement of restrictive covenants on properties within the Village. The restrictive covenants require the Village's approval if a transfer of title would cause (1) the removal of the property from the Village's tax rolls; (2) a reduction in the tax value; or 3) the removal of the property from the Village's zoning authority and zoning jurisdiction. A potential purchaser can avoid the requirement to obtain Village consent by agreeing to pay real estate taxes and to abide by the Village's zoning authority. When individuals have their property surveyed for subdivisions, the Village requires that they place these restrictive covenants on the property as part of the approval process. Only the Village of Hobart can take action to rescind the covenants.

These restrictive covenants are a clear attempt to prevent the Nation from acquiring land and having the land taken into trust status. When a golf course with these restrictive covenants became available for purchase during a pending bankruptcy, the Nation worked with the bank holding the loans to remove the restrictive covenants. Unfortunately, the court did not agree and essentially told the Nation that if it did not like the restrictive covenants, it should not purchase the property. Moving to Plan B, the Nation passed a resolution that satisfied the conditions of the restrictive covenants. Despite the Nation's efforts, the Village still objected to the transfer, but the court rejected the Village's attempts to stop the sale of the land to the Nation.[3] The Nation purchased the property shortly thereafter and undertook a public relations campaign to inform nontribal citizens who owned homes surrounding the golf course that the Nation would continue the level of customer service and professionalism that had prevailed at the facility. Where tribal laws would apply, those laws met and often exceeded state standards. In turn, the nontribal citizens generally supported the Nation's acquisition and continued to frequent the golf course, restaurant, bar, and banquet hall located on the property.

BACKGROUND

In 1992 Jack and Carol Schweiner began developing a golf course and subdivision on land they owned on the Oneida reservation.[4] Over the years, they continued to acquire more land and developed the expanding golf course and surrounding subdivision. After a dispute with a substantial investor ended up in court, the golf course went into receivership, and the Village of Hobart purchased it in 2003. The Village then leased the property back to a newly formed Thornberry Creek Golf Course, LLC (TCGC), run by Jack and Carol Schweiner. Under the terms of the lease, in 2005 TCGC was able to reacquire the property. The 2005 transfer included two other simultaneous provisions. The first was a right of first refusal by which the Village retained the right to reacquire the property if TCGC were to sell. Second was the creation of a restrictive covenant. This restrictive covenant would later form the basis of the dispute at hand. The first of the relevant sections of the restrictive covenant is as follows:

> Restriction on Transfer. Without the express written consent of the Village of Hobart, no owner of any interest in the Subject Real Estate . . . shall transfer any interest in the Subject Real Estate to any individual, entity, . . . or sovereign nation, or during the period of ownership take any action the result of which would:
>
> (1) remove or eliminate the Subject Real Estate (or any part thereof) from the tax rolls of the Village of Hobart;
>
> (2) diminish or eliminate the payment of real estate taxes levied or assessed against the Subject Real Estate (or any part thereof) and/or
>
> (3) remove the Subject Real Estate (or any part thereof) from the zoning authority and/or jurisdiction of the Village of Hobart.[5]

Other provisions of the restrictive covenants required the Village to waive the consent requirement if a purchaser met certain requirements. The tax provision was subject to waiver if a tax-exempt purchaser agreed to make payments in lieu of taxes, and the zoning provision was subject to waiver if the purchaser delivered to the Village "a legally enforceable consent agreement whereby the owner or proposed transferee agrees to be bound by the . . . zoning authority and/or jurisdiction of the Village." In 2007 TCGC and the Schweiners again found themselves in financial trouble and filed for Chapter 11 bankruptcy relief. At that time, Baylake Bank held the mortgages on the golf course and some of the Schweiners' personal property and had a financial interest in settling the bankruptcy. A cash sale to the Oneida Nation offered a quick and clean solution. During the bankruptcy proceedings, the Oneida Nation proposed to acquire the property and entered into a purchase agreement with TCGC that was conditioned on removal of the restrictive covenants, among other things. As a result, the bank filed a lawsuit challenging the legitimacy of the restrictive covenants and argued that the covenants were void under state and federal law. This would become the first round of litigation surrounding the proposed sale of the golf course to the Nation.

On June 28, 2008, the General Tribal Council (GTC) met to discuss the purchase. There were 1,190 tribal citizens at the meeting. This purchase would add more than three hundred acres to the Nation's land base. The late Amelia Cornelius, then chairwoman of the Oneida Land Commission, commented on how much land this would add to the Nation's land base: "It's 325 acres in Hobart. We currently have 5,000 acres in Hobart, percentagewise, that's 2 percent of tribal land."[6] The tribal citizens wanted to deliver a message to the Village that the Nation would not change course because of the Village's attempts to keep the land out of the hands of the Nation. One Oneida elder, Hugh Danforth, spoke out at the meeting, explaining, "All Hobart wants us to do is disappear. This is a good opportunity."[7]

Another vein of discussion arose during the meeting concerning the acquisition of a business. My uncle Gerald Doxtator spoke about the failing golf course, explaining, "It's a business that's failing. If it was making money, it wouldn't be in bankruptcy. We need to look at the economy. We're going to have to keep that sinking boat afloat."[8] While individual citizens may have had a multitude of reasons for voting one way or the other, those citizens who spoke up during the meeting were far more likely to speak about the opportunity to reacquire land than to talk about the business. After a lengthy discussion, the GTC overwhelmingly passed a resolution titled, "Support of Purchase of Thornberry Creek Country Club and Golf Course and Related Properties in Bankruptcy Court."[9] The message was clear: although the business was failing, the land was more important.

ROUND 1 OF LITIGATION

During this first round of litigation, Baylake Bank challenged the restrictive covenants used by the Village to block the sale of the property to the Oneida Nation. In doing so, the bank's attorneys presented a number of legal arguments. The primary argument was that the covenants constituted impermissible restraints on alienation under state law. This argument was based on an interpretation of the covenants as requiring the Village's consent to any transfer. Two other arguments that weren't presented to the court are discussed here.

Fee-to-Trust

In 1934, Congress passed the Indian Reorganization Act (IRA).[10] One of the goals of the Act was to help restore tribal land bases by acquiring land for tribal governments and individual tribal citizens. The IRA specifically authorizes the secretary of the interior to acquire, without the consent of the state, "any interest in lands, water rights, or surface rights to lands within or without existing Indian reservations" through purchase, gift, or exchange "for the purpose of providing land for Indians."[11] The Code of Federal Regulations sets forth a number of factors the secretary must consider when deciding whether to take land into trust.[12] Consent of state or municipal governments is not among the factors.

The Oneida Nation has an ambitious goal of reacquiring all the land on the Oneida reservation and restoring that land to trust status. Assigning trust status means that title to the land is held by the United States for the benefit of the Nation and that the land is removed from the local tax rolls; it also clears up jurisdictional questions related to condemnation and land use regulations. Since trust acquisition by the United States would remove the land from the Village's tax rolls, under the restrictive covenants the Nation would not be able to have the land placed into trust status without the Village's consent. Because of the hostile relationship between the Village government and the Nation and the Village's vocal objections to the Nation's efforts to have land taken into trust status, the Nation understood that it would not be able to secure the Village's consent. As a result, the restrictive covenants would essentially prevent the Nation or individual Nation citizens from having the land taken into trust status unless the Nation or individual agreed to make payments in lieu of taxes and the Nation or individual and the secretary of the interior agreed that the property would be subject to the Village's zoning authority after trust acquisition.[13]

The real-life consequence of such restrictive covenants is that they severely complicate the efforts of an average Oneida Nation citizen to have fee land subject to the restrictive covenants taken into trust status. While such a covenant would not be an absolute bar to trust acquisitions, it would hinder the process laid out in the Indian Reorganization Act of 1934, established for the express purpose of helping Indians rebuild their land bases. Having to reacquire their own land and then to continue to pay taxes or the equivalent of taxes on that land indefinitely despite the fact that the Nation provides governmental services to Nation citizens and nontribal members alike imposes an economic burden on tribal citizens and the Nation as a whole.

Regulatory Framework of the IRA's Fee-To-Trust Process

Baylake Bank argued that Congress enacted a comprehensive regulatory framework governing the fee-to-trust process that preempted state or municipal action that interfered with that process. Baylake Bank also argued that the Village's restrictive covenants impaired the Nation's right, granted under federal law, to purchase the land and to have that land taken into trust status. That, in turn, interfered with the federal government's ability to meet its trust obligations to Indian tribes. Enforcement of the restrictive covenants would therefore be preempted by federal law as set forth in the IRA.

The issue ended up before the United States District Court for the Eastern District of Wisconsin. The court was not persuaded by Baylake Bank's arguments, declined to find the restrictive covenants void or unenforceable, and declined to find anything in the restrictive covenants that violated the Nation's right to have land taken into trust. The court explained: "The procedures espoused in the IRA and its regulations do not somehow create an underlying 'right' to apply for trust status, and they certainly do not invest in tribes the 'right' to purchase any land within their reservations and then have that land placed in trust. . . . Such a result would grant a quasi-property right to tribes over any land within the boundaries of their reservations."[14] In short, the court essentially said if the Nation didn't like the restrictive covenants, it shouldn't purchase the property.

The Nation Consents to the Village's Zoning

After receiving the decision that the restrictive covenants were valid, the Nation had to reconsider its options. Since acquiring the property in the Nation's name would not remove the property from the tax rolls or diminish the payment of real estate taxes levied, the Nation did not need to address the tax issue. However, the Nation's long-standing position has been that once it reacquires land in fee status on the Oneida reservation, that land becomes subject to the Nation's zoning laws and is removed from the zoning jurisdiction of state and municipal governments.[15] Accordingly, the Nation's acquisition of the land would trigger the consent agreement requirement with respect to the zoning clause. In a footnote to one of its briefs, Baylake Bank explained: "It appears that fee ownership of the property by the Tribe may remove the parcel from the Village's zoning authority and jurisdiction. This issue is not before the Court, and the Court need not consider this issue."[16]

Faced with deciding how to move forward with the acquisition of the golf course in light of the questions regarding zoning jurisdiction over fee land, the Nation decided to agree to abide by the Village's zoning authority and zoning jurisdiction with respect to the golf course. By the terms of the restrictive covenants, if the Nation agreed to be bound by the Village's zoning authority and zoning jurisdiction, the Village's consent would not be necessary for the sale of the property to the Nation. On October 30, 2008, the Nation executed a tribal resolution consenting to that jurisdiction and providing a limited waiver of tribal sovereign immunity.[17] The relevant provisions of the resolution are as follows:

NOW THEREFORE BE IT RESOLVED, with respect to only those portions of the Property subject to the Restrictive Covenants, and only for so long as those Restrictive Covenants remain in place, the Oneida Business Committee agrees to comply with and be subject to the Village of Hobart's zoning authority and zoning jurisdiction as set forth in duly adopted Village of Hobart zoning Ordinances; and

NOW THEREFORE BE IT FURTHER RESOLVED, with respect to only those portions of the Property subject to the Restrictive Covenants, and only for so long as those Restrictive Covenants remain in place, the Oneida Business Committee hereby grants a limited waiver of sovereign immunity in favor of the Village of Hobart to permit the Village of Hobart to enforce its duly adopted zoning ordinances against the Tribe; and

NOW THEREFORE BE IT FURTHER RESOLVED, prior to such time as the Restrictive Covenants may be removed from the Property, the Tribe will not, without the consent of the Village of Hobart, revoke either the Tribe's consent to be subject to the Village of Hobart's zoning authority and zoning jurisdiction, or the Tribe's limited waiver of sovereign immunity to allow the Village of Hobart to enforce its duly adopted zoning ordinances against the Tribe, with respect to, but only with respect to, the portion of the Property subject to the Restrictive Covenants.

For me, consenting to the Village's zoning jurisdiction within the reservation boundaries was a hard pill to swallow. Part of the purpose of reacquiring land within our boundaries is to be able to determine, as a Nation, how to make the best use of that land. Consenting to the Village's zoning jurisdiction took that consent away and forced the Nation to continue to use the property how the Village wanted it to be used.

Round 2 of Litigation

Despite the Nation's agreement to abide by the Village's zoning authority and zoning jurisdiction, the Village still tried to block the sale, and Baylake Bank and the Village found themselves in a second round of litigation. The Village advanced two arguments this time around. First, it argued that the sale of the property to the Nation would ultimately result in removal of the property from the tax rolls because the Nation had repeatedly stated its intent to apply to have the land taken into trust. Second, it maintained that the consent and waiver were not broad enough because they did not subject the Nation to the Village's general jurisdiction. The Village also claimed it was not adequately protected and needed a broader waiver of tribal sovereign immunity. The Bankruptcy Court determined that the waiver was sufficient, and the Village appealed to the Eastern District of Wisconsin. The following is an excerpt from the Eastern District Court's decision rejecting the Village's appeal.

> The Village also appeals the bankruptcy court's conclusion that the Tribe's limited waiver of immunity for zoning purposes was sufficient to protect the Village's interest. In addition to the restrictions on removing the property from the tax rolls, the covenant provides in Section 1(3) that no owner shall take any action that would "remove the Subject Real Estate (or any part thereof) from the zoning authority and/or jurisdiction of the Village of Hobart." The parties agreed that the transfer to the Oneida *would* trigger this clause (unlike the clause relating to taxes) because tribal ownership of the land (which is within the reservation's boundaries) would arguably remove the land from the Village's zoning authority. The covenant provides an "out," however: the Village's consent requirement is to be waived as to Section 1(3) "upon receipt of a legally enforceable consent agreement whereby the owner or proposed transferee agrees to be bound by the whereby the [*sic*] zoning authority and/or jurisdiction of the Village."
>
> To this end, the Oneida provided a limited waiver of sovereign immunity. It agreed to comply with and be subject to the Village's "zoning authority and zoning jurisdiction as set forth in duly adopted Village of Hobart zoning ordinances." It further agreed to waive its sovereign immunity with respect to enforcement of the agreement to comply with and be subject to the Village's zoning authority and zoning jurisdiction.[18]

The court rejected the Village's appeal and held that the Nation's consent agreement adequately resolved any issues raised in covenants.[19] This last attempt to prevent the Nation from acquiring the golf course, even though the Nation's acquisition would not remove the property from the tax rolls and the Nation followed the provisions of the restrictive covenants and agreed to be bound by Village's zoning authority, suggests the Village simply did not want the Nation to own the golf course.

Conflicting Grammar Interpretations in the Covenants

One side note within this litigation is a dispute over the meaning of a phrase in the covenants. The covenants refer to "zoning authority and/or jurisdiction of the Village of Hobart." When the Nation passed the tribal resolution and agreed to the Village's zoning authority in order to remove the requirement for village consent under the restrictive covenants, the Nation specifically agreed to be bound by "the Village of Hobart's zoning authority and zoning jurisdiction."

In an attempt to assert more jurisdiction over the Nation, the Village claimed the word "zoning" modified only the word "authority" and not the word "jurisdiction." Essentially, the Village wanted the court to interpret this provision of the restrictive covenant to require a purchaser to be bound by the Village's zoning authority and general jurisdiction. In short, the Village wanted a broader consent and waiver of immunity from the Nation with respect to the Village's general jurisdiction over matters unrelated to the land itself. The Village wanted the Nation to come under the Village's general jurisdiction, as would typical landowners. Fortunately, the Court did not agree with the demand for such a broad waiver over matters that have nothing whatsoever to do with the land.

Closing Observations

In December 2008, the Nation acquired TCGC. I remember driving with the late Rick Hill, then chairman of the Oneida Nation, in a pickup truck the night of the closing. A blizzard was about to pass through, and the roads were already getting slick. Despite the deteriorating conditions, Rick wanted us to drive a "victory lap" around TCGC. So we did. I remember Rick's booming laugh as we drove through the snowy roads. He kept repeating that "we did it" and that our grandchildren would not have to worry about reacquiring this property because it was ours now and we will protect it.

Since the reacquisition of golf course, the Nation has hosted the Ladies Professional Golf Association tournament for three years; the tournament was broadcast on national and international television and brought thousands of visitors to the area. The Nation has hosted a junior golf program, exposing hundreds of Oneida youth to the sport. The golf course also welcomed a number of tournaments and fundraisers as well as weddings and parties, the Miss Oneida pageant, and concerts by Native American bands. This exposure of Oneida contemporary life allows nontribal employees and customers to interact with Oneida citizens in a nonpolitical setting, helping to break down stereotypes and strengthening interpersonal relationships among all reservation residents.

Of course, the Village holds this case out as a victory for preserving its restrictive covenants and preventing more land from being removed from the tax rolls. Similarly, the Nation holds this case out as a victory because the Nation now owns TCGC despite the Village's attempts to prevent the Nation from acquiring it. It should come as no surprise that I agree with the latter perspective and count this case as a victory for the Nation. The Nation now owns the property and is looking to a longer-term goal of outlasting current Village of Hobart politics. Politics are temporary; Nation ownership of the land is forever.

Notes

1. See chap. 2 for a discussion about the allotment acts.

2. See chap. 9 for a broader discussion about what trust status means, why the Oneida Nation wants to have its land taken into trust status, and why the Village opposes the fee-to-trust process.

3. The Village of Hobart v. TCGC, LLC, Baylake Bank and Oneida Tribe, 08-MC-59 (E. Dis. Wis. 2008).

4. Baylake Bank v. TCGC, LLC, Case No. 08-C-608, E.D. Wis. Brief in Support of Plaintiff's Motion for Summary Judgment.

5. Brown County Register of Deeds, March 22, 2005, Document No. 2179285.

6. Oneida General Tribal Council meeting minutes, June 28, 2008, 8.

7. Oneida General Tribal Council meeting minutes, 1.

8. Oneida General Tribal Council meeting minutes, 6.

9. General Tribal Council Resolution GTC-6-28-08-A.

10. 25 U.S.C. §465 et. Seq.

11. 25 U.S.C. §465.

12. 25 C.F.R. §151.

13. See 25 CFR 1.4, under which the secretary of the interior may agree that certain properties or areas remain subject to municipal zoning after trust acquisition.

14. Baylake Bank v. TCGC, LLC, 2008 U.S. Dist. LEXIS 77291; 2008 WL 4525009, 22–23.

15. The law is more settled with respect to the zoning of trust land than with respect to the zoning of fee land. Compare Gobin v. Snohomish, 304 F.3d 909 (9th Cir. 2002) with Seneca-Cayuga Tribe of Oklahoma v. Town of Aurelius, New York, 233 F.R.D. 278 (N.D.N.Y. 2006).

16. Baylake Bank v. TCGC, LLC, Case No. 08-C-608, E.D. Wis. Brief in Support of Plaintiff's Motion for Summary Judgment, Footnote 8. Citing Gobin v. Snohomish, 304 F.3d 909 (9th Cir. 2002).

17. Oneida Business Committee Resolution BC-10-30-08-A.

18. Village of Hobart v. TCGC, LLC, 2008 U.S. Dist. LEXIS 105468; 2008 WL 5377911, 5. Internal citations omitted. Quotes are from an affidavit from the Village's attorney, David Cisar.

19. Village of Hobart v. TCGC, LLC, 10.

CHAPTER 7

─────────────── ❧ ───────────────

Stormwater Taxes

"Anyway There Are No Tribal Debts to Hobart"

REBECCA M. WEBSTER

KEY TERMS IN THIS CHAPTER

- Fee-to-trust
- Real estate taxation
- Tribal sovereign immunity

In 2007 the Village adopted an ordinance and began imposing charges for stormwater management on all land within the Village, including the Nation's trust land. The Nation refused to pay the charges levied against the Nation's trust property. As described in chapter 7, the Nation operates a golf course with a bar and restaurant in the Village, and the Village threatened to withhold the Nation's liquor license if it didn't pay the stormwater charges.

After the Nation declined to pay the charges levied against trust land for two years, the Nation and the Village entered into an escrow agreement under which the Village agreed to issue a liquor license for the golf course and the Nation agreed to deposit the disputed charges in an escrow account while the Nation and the Village attempted to resolve the disputed charges, including through litigation if necessary. Pursuant to the escrow agreement, the parties agreed that if they could not resolve the dispute, they would both waive sovereign and/or governmental immunity for the limited purpose of obtaining a judicial determination of the Village's authority to impose its charges on the Nation's trust land.

The Nation and the Village met to attempt to resolve the dispute but were unable to do so. The Nation then filed suit in the United States District Court for the Eastern District of Wisconsin, asking the court to declare that the Village does not have the authority to impose stormwater charges against the Nation's trust property. The Village filed an answer and counterclaims against the Nation and eventually also filed a third-party complaint against the United States. The Nation moved for summary judgment on its first two claims for relief, and the United States moved for dismissal of the third-party complaint. In 2012, the court ruled that the charges are taxes and are precluded by federal law. The Village appealed. In 2013, the Seventh Circuit Court of Appeals upheld the decision. The Village petitioned for review by the United States Supreme Court. The Supreme Court denied the Village's petition.

BACKGROUND

Nation's Water Quality Regulations

The Nation has promulgated ordinances that comprehensively regulate water quality on the Oneida reservation, including stormwater run-off on its trust land. The Oneida Code of Laws includes Chapter 69, the Zoning and Shoreland Protection Law, adopted in 1981 to prevent surface water run-off into creeks and wetlands; Chapter 46, the On-Site Waste Disposal Ordinance, adopted in 1988 to regulate private sewage systems; Chapter 47, the Sanitation Ordinance, adopted in 1990 to regulate water and sanitary utilities; Chapter 43, the Well Abandonment Law, adopted in 1994 to require the abandonment or upgrade of unused, unsafe, or noncomplying wells; Chapter 48, the Water Resources Ordinance, adopted in 1996 to regulate present and potential sources of water pollution; and Chapter 41, the Non-Metallic Mining Ordinance, adopted in 2007 to regulate reclamation projects for the purpose of meeting water quality standards for surface waters and wetlands.

The Nation has an Environmental, Health and Safety Division (the "Division") which is tasked with implementation and enforcement of the Nation's environmental laws and programs. At the time of the dispute, the Division had an annual budget of approximately $3.7 million.

Within the Division, seven staff members were assigned to the Water Resources Team, which was responsible for carrying out the Nation's water quality programs. The Nation expended approximately $800,000 annually for water quality programs that were directly or indirectly related to mitigating the effects of stormwater run-off. Specific activities included restoring and enhancing meanders to streams and creeks to slow the flow of water, restoring and enhancing wetlands to provide for filtration of stormwater, establishing buffer zones between agricultural fields and waterways, planting cover vegetation to control erosion, investigating and responding to spills, monitoring water quality for both point and non-point sources of pollution, constructing site erosion control, and sponsoring community education regarding best practices to reduce pollution to waterways and improve water quality. In addition to these efforts, the Nation installed and maintains on-site stormwater treatment facilities on tribal properties, including water infiltration systems and retention ponds.

The Nation has entered into a Direct Implementation Tribal Co-operative Agreement with the United States Environmental Protection Agency (EPA) for the control of stormwater runoff from construction sites, and employees of the Nation have received federal credentials with respect to construction site permitting and investigation under the Clean Water Act and related regulations.

Village's Stormwater Ordinance and Charges

In 2007 the Nation had approximately 1,420 acres of trust land situated on the Oneida reservation and in the Village.[1] Starting in July 2007, the Village began imposing a "fee" on all property located within the Village, including the Nation's trust property, for the alleged purpose of managing stormwater run-off. The Village imposed these "fees" under its Stormwater Utility Management Ordinance (the "Ordinance"), which created a Storm Water Management Utility to assess and impose "fees" on all real property located in the Village.[2] Pursuant to the Ordinance, unpaid charges "shall be a lien upon the property served."[3] The Ordinance further provided that the Village would collect delinquent charges pursuant to state laws concerning tax levies and tax foreclosure.[4]

On January 31, 2008, the Nation sent a letter to the Village explaining that the charges were invalid under federal law and declining to pay the charges.[5] The Village took no action with respect to the charges. In December 2008, the Village once again imposed the charges under the Ordinance on the Nation's trust property. By letter dated January 14, 2009, the Nation again declined to pay the charges levied against the Nation's trust property.

While all this was going on, the Oneida Golf Enterprise Corporation ("OEGC"), a tribally chartered corporation wholly owned by the Nation, was operating Thornberry Creek at Oneida, the golf course discussed in chapter 7 of this book. OEGC served alcohol in its clubhouse and on the golf course grounds. Pursuant to federal law, Congress delegated the authority to regulate liquor sales on reservations to the states.[6] The State of Wisconsin further delegated this responsibility to municipalities.[7] The Village attempted to leverage this authority by threatening to withhold a liquor license to OEGC if the Nation did not pay the stormwater charges levied against the Nation's trust property.[8] On March 25, 2009, to avoid disruptions to the OEGC's operations, the Nation entered into an escrow agreement with the Village under which the Nation agreed to pay the disputed charges into an escrow account and the Village agreed to issue a liquor license to OEGC. The escrow agreement provided a ninety-day window for the Nation and the Village to resolve the dispute, after which either party could seek judicial resolution of the dispute.

On March 24, 2009, the Bureau of Indian Affairs (BIA) Midwest Regional Office sent a letter to the Village and the Nation regarding the Village's charges on trust property. The letter advised the Nation and the Village that the charges constituted a tax and that taxes may not be imposed on land held in trust by the United States. The BIA requested the Village to immediately delete the Nation's trust land from the tax certificate and to terminate further collection action. Again, the Village did not take any action to remove the charges. On December 15, 2009, the Nation received the 2009 annual tax bills for its fee and trust land. The bills included amounts levied by the Village for the charges under the Ordinance for the Nation's trust land, notwithstanding direction to the contrary from the BIA.

Litigation

Pursuant to the terms of the escrow agreement, the Nation and the Village met to resolve the dispute over the charges levied against the Nation's trust property. The Village and the Nation were unable to reach a resolution. As stipulated in the escrow agreement, the parties agreed that if they were unable to reach an agreement, they would waive sovereign/government immunity and have the issue heard before a federal court. On February 19, 2010, the Nation filed a complaint for declaratory and injunctive relief in the United States District Court for the Eastern District of Wisconsin. The complaint asked the court to declare the Nation's trust property immune to the Village's stormwater charges and to affirm that the Village lacked the authority to impose the charges on the Nation's trust property. The complaint also requested an order from the court that would prevent the Village from imposing or collecting the charges levied against the Nation's trust property. The complaint advanced three main arguments. First, the Village's stormwater charges are a tax on trust land, and federal law provides that trust land is not subject to taxation. Second, even if the charge is deemed to be a fee, the charges are still impermissible because the Nation's trust land is subject to comprehensive federal regulations and the Village's stormwater charges interfere with those federal regulations. Third, the Nation has the inherent right to self-government and the Village's stormwater charges interfere with the Nation's right to self-government.

In response, the Village filed an answer and asserted a number of counterclaims dealing with the Nation's status as a federally recognized tribe, the continuing existence of the Oneida reservation, and the ability of the secretary of the interior to take land into trust for tribes. The Village also claimed it had the authority to impose the stormwater charges as a matter of federal and state law. The Nation's arguments and the Village's arguments are outlined in the following sections.

Nation's Claims

The Nation advanced three main arguments when it filed its complaint to protect its trust land from the stormwater charges and potential tax foreclosure action. First, the Nation argued that the Village's storm-water charges constituted an impermissible tax on the land. Federal law provides that trust land is not taxable. The Indian Reorganization Act authorizes the secretary of the interior to place land into trust to be held by the United States for the benefit of Indian tribes, and such lands "shall be exempt from State and local taxation."[9] In addition, pursuant to the Indian Reorganization Act, the secretary of the interior has promulgated regulations that prohibit local regulation and taxation of trust lands.[10] Imposition of the charges, the Nation argued, violated the tax immunity provided for those lands by federal law and regulation.

Second, the Nation argued that the Village's stormwater ordinance was preempted by federal law. Under federal common law and rules governing construction of Indian statutes, federal law preempts the application of state and local law and regulations to recognized Indian tribes and their property located in Indian country when federal regulation is comprehensive.[11] Federal regulation of the Nation's trust property is comprehensive and pervasive and precludes state and local regulation by virtue of the Supremacy Clause of the United States Constitution.[12] Regardless of whether the Village's stormwater charges constituted a tax on the trust land, the Nation argued that the charges were preempted by the pervasive and comprehensive federal regulation of the Nation's trust land.

Third, the Nation argued the Village's stormwater ordinance violated the Nation's inherent right to self-government. This right to self-government includes the authority to manage and regulate the Oneida reservation and tribal property, including tribal trust land. In the exercise of its inherent power of self-government, the Nation has promulgated tribal law to manage the water resources on the Oneida reservation, including stormwater run-off on trust lands. The Nation's interests in the regulation of its trust land, including stormwater run-off, far outweigh any interest the Village has in regulating the same land for the same purpose. Similarly, the overriding federal policy and law is to protect the Nation's inherent power of self-government. The federal interests in encouraging tribal self-sufficiency and economic development with particular reference to the Nation's trust lands far outweigh any interest the

Village has in regulating the Nation's trust land. Regardless of whether the Village's stormwater charges constituted a tax on the trust land, the Village's attempts to levy their stormwater charges on tribal trust property violated the Nation's inherent powers of self-government.

Village's Counterclaim

In response to the Nation's complaint, the Village filed a counterclaim and advanced a number of affirmative defenses. The Village's two primary affirmative defenses centered around the status of trust land and the Oneida reservation. The Village pled novel theories challenging existing federal Indian law regarding the secretary of the interior's authority to take land into trust and the alleged disestablishment of Indian reservations.

First, the Village asserted that the land was not properly held in trust.[13] According to the Village, the Oneida Nation was not under federal jurisdiction in 1934, when Congress passed the Indian Reorganization Act, and therefore was ineligible to have land taken into trust status. The Village based this argument on the Supreme Court's decision in *Carcieri v. Salazar*.[14] In that case, SCOTUS held that only recognized tribes that were under federal jurisdiction in 1934 are eligible to have land taken into trust status under the Indian Reorganization Act. If a tribe was not under federal jurisdiction in 1934, it is ineligible to have land taken into trust status. Alternatively, the Village argued even if the Nation was under federal jurisdiction, the secretary of the interior lacked authority to remove land from state jurisdiction because "there is no federal authority to nullify state jurisdiction."[15] The Village further challenged the constitutionality of federal regulations that clarify that state and local regulations do not apply to trust land.[16] The Village claimed that those federal regulations deprive the Village of its authority to enforce its stormwater ordinance and "wrongfully deprive[ ] the state and Village the right to fully participate in their governance."[17]

Second, with respect to the status of the reservation, the Village advanced a misguided interpretation of the 1838 treaty that created the reservation. The portion of the treaty establishing the Oneida reservation reads as follows: "there shall be reserved to the said Indians to be held as other Indian lands are held a tract of land containing one hundred (100) acres, for each individual, and the lines of which shall be so run as to include all their settlements and improvements in the vicinity of Green Bay."[18] The Village erroneously claimed the treaty called for the allotment of land to individual tribal members and created a temporary reservation that soon disappeared.

In addition to filing counterclaims against the Nation, the Village also filed a third-party complaint against the United States because the land at issue was held in trust by the United States. In its third-party complaint, the Village claimed it suffered losses and demanded the United States pay the stormwater charges that the Nation had refused to pay. The Village claimed that state and federal law required it to implement a stormwater management ordinance and collect charges and that the Village was compelled to collect fees from landowners, including the Nation and the United States.[19] The Village further claimed that the Clean Water Act directed the United States to comply with the Village's Stormwater Ordinance relating to the control of water pollution, including charges levied to fund the Village's stormwater program. These arguments reflected a profound misunderstanding of the Clean Water Act's stormwater management provisions as granting stormwater permit holders authority to exercise jurisdiction that they do not possess, when in fact permit holders are regulated entities and must comply with the Clean Water Act's stormwater provisions by utilizing their existing authority. The arguments also were entirely beside the point, as the Village did not possess a stormwater permit.

Court's Decision

In 2012 the Eastern District of Wisconsin issued a decision in this case. The court determined that the fee was a tax and that the Clean Water Act did not give the Village permission to tax the Nation's trust property or to demand that the United States pay any taxes. The court held "that the Tribe's trust land is immune from the Village's Storm Water Management Utility Ordinance and that the Village lacks authority to impose charges under the Ordinance on the Tribe's land directly or indirectly. The judgment shall also enjoin the Village from attempting to impose and collect 'charges' under the Ordinance from the Tribe or from foreclosing on the Tribe's lands."[20] The court also noted the long-standing differences between the Nation and the Village and expressed the following view: "The plain fact, however, is that the interests of the Village and the Tribe are not aligned; their constituencies are not the same and they have vastly different plans for the future. As a result, cooperation is more difficult. But this does not change the law."[21]

The Village appealed the decision to the Seventh Circuit Court of Appeals. In 2013 that court affirmed the district court's decision in favor of the Nation. In the decision, the court of appeals commented on the overall process of taking land into trust. It noted how tribes acquire land in their own name and then apply to have that land taken into trust status. In doing so, the United States government acts as a trustee of tribal trust lands. The court distinguished this from a situation in which the federal government simply donated land to tribes. The court of appeals explained, "The government's status as trustee rather than merely donor of tribal lands is designed to preserve tribal sovereignty, not to make the federal government pay tribal debts. Anyway there are no tribal debts to Hobart."[22] This last sentence responds to a huge misconception in the non-Indian world about what trust status of land means. To me, the inclusion of this sentence as the final word meant that the court of appeals recognized the Nation as a legitimate government with rights and responsibilities to its community and its citizens. The court did not paint the Nation as the Village would have it, a common landowner subject to all Village regulations.

The Village filed a petition for certiorari asking SCOTUS to review the Seventh Circuit's decision. SCOTUS declined to hear their appeal.

CLOSING OBSERVATIONS

During the appeal of this case, the Village held an election to fill two seats on the Village Board. The two incumbents that held those seats and were running for re-election were facing a new challenger, Mike Hoeft, a non-tribal member married to an Oneida tribal member who also served on the Oneida Business Committee. A month before the election, Village President Rich Heidel stuffed a letter in the mailboxes of many Village residents. Not surprisingly, he missed our mailbox and the mailboxes of most tribal members I talked to. Although he signed the letter in his official capacity as Village president, he did not use Village letterhead. In the letter, Heidel vilified the Nation. The following is an excerpt:

> Most importantly, this body has been, and still is, Hobart's adversary in a number of legal actions—some initiated by the Tribe and some by the Village, but all of which deal with the Tribe's challenge to the authority and jurisdiction of the Village of Hobart, its residents, and by extension, Brown County and the state of Wisconsin. . . . *Neither I nor you should be fooled or intimidated into thinking that Mike is anything but the spouse of a dedicated Tribal official with an agenda that runs deeply counter to the best interests of you as a taxpayer, as a property owner, and as a citizen of the village of Hobart.*
>
> *Your votes for Dave Dillenburg and Donna Severson are essential* in order for the Village to continue protecting your rights, enhancing your property values, and securing the future for ALL of our citizens, both enrolled Tribal members and non-tribal alike.[23]

At least one of the judges of the United States Court of Appeals for the Seventh Circuit saw a copy of this letter and brought it up during oral arguments. The judge asked the Village's attorney about Heidel's letter and how tribal members are treated, or rather, excluded. Another judge (Judge 2) mentioned that the letter was insensitive.

JUDGE 1: Hobart doesn't seem to like Indians, right?
KOWALKOWSKI: I don't think that's true at all your honor.
JUDGE 1: What about the letter from Heidel?
KOWALKOWSKI: I, I think Hobart's position. . . .
JUDGE 1: The March letter from Heidel about the spouse of the dedicated tribal official with an agenda that runs counter to the best interest to you as a tax payer. You endorse that letter? Is that proper—
KOWALKOWSKI: Your honor,
JUDGE 1:—statement to all Hobart friends, neighbors, and constituents?
KOWALKOWSKI: Your honor, I don't have the letter—

JUDGE 1: You know what the letter says.

KOWALKOWSKI: I do in general, yes.

JUDGE 1: What do you mean in general? You know what the letter is. I just read you the relevant portion. Is that a proper attitude?

KOWALKOWSKI: The attitude is to preserve Hobart's jurisdiction as it sees it is entitled to do. And it's trying to protect its elected government and the laws it believes it has under the constitution.

JUDGE 1: Do you approve of the letter?

KOWALKOWSKI: I don't approve or disapprove of the letter, your honor. I didn't draft it. I wasn't involved in it.

JUDGE 1: What do you mean you didn't draft it? I'm not asking you whether you drafted it. I want to know if you think this is a proper way to deal with the Indians or improper way.

KOWALKOWSKI: I think the concern was legitimate because it had to do with a—

JUDGE 1: What about the expression of the concern?

[inaudible]

JUDGE 2: Perhaps its [sic] insensitive in a way.

KOWALKOWSKI: Perhaps the sensitivity level—

JUDGE 3: There you go.

KOWALKOWSKI: I would agree, the sensitivity level could have been maybe worded in a less adversarial tone. But I think the core concern of having tribal representatives, you know, impacting Hobart's decision making process and some of the conflicts and closed session issues.

JUDGE 1: Why is that? You want to tax the Indians, but you don't want them to have anything to do with the government of Hobart? I don't understand.

KOWALKOWSKI: Hobart's not taking the position that—

JUDGE 1: They don't have any voice in the—

KOWALKOWSKI: They certainly do and they can absolutely run for office.

JUDGE 1: Why is he so concerned about the fact that the wife of one of the Village officials is an Indian?

KOWALKOWSKI: Because he was concerned with going into closed session and having other discussions with issues relating to negotiations with the Nation or litigation with the Nation.

JUDGE 1: How are the Indians different from the other residents of Hobart?

KOWALKOWSKI: Well, your, your typical other resident's most likely not going to be involved in litigation.[24]

Immediately after Kowalkowski's last statement, one of the judges redirected the conversation back to the litigation at hand. While the fact that a judge brought this up during oral arguments surprised me, the sentiment in Heidel's letter did not. I grew up on the portion of the reservation that hosted the Village. During my time as an attorney for the Nation, I also resided on that portion of the reservation as well. I was a taxpaying citizen. Whenever tribal members attended Village meetings, Heidel and the other Board members made sure to point us out. During one meeting in particular, Kowalkowski was about to give an update on litigation to the citizens in attendance. Before he could start, Heidel loudly proclaimed, while looking directly at me, "Be careful what you say in here, we have spies among us." As shocking as this may be, it's not nearly as shocking as the statement he made during another meeting to a tribal member colleague of mine. He pointed at her and proclaimed that the Village would be "the point man on the rifle squad" in battles with the Nation.[25]

NOTES

1. Oneida Nation's Complaint for Declaratory and Injunctive Relief. Oneida Tribe of Indians of Wisconsin v. Village of Hobart, 891 F.Supp.2d 1058, 1071 (E.D. Wis. 2012).

2. Ordinances, §§4.501 Findings, 4.508 Billing and Penalties; Ordinance, §4.505(4) Rates and Charges.

3. Ordinance, §4.508(3) Billing and Penalties.

4. Ordinance, §4.508(3) Billing and Penalties. This section states, "The Village shall collect delinquent charges under Wis. Stat. §§66.0821(4) and 66.0809(3)." State law specifically provided that "arrears and penalty will be levied as a tax against the lot or parcel of real estate." The statute further authorizes the use of the same proceedings "in relation to the collection of general property taxes and to the return and sale of property for delinquent taxes." Wis. Statm. §66.0809(3).

5. Oneida Nation's Complaint for Declaratory and Injunctive Relief.

6. 18 U.S.C. §1161.

7. Wis. Stat. Sec. 125.25, 125.26.

8. Village Ordinance Section 189-6 states, in relevant part, "The issuance of all licenses, whether an original or renewal, are subject to the Village Board's discretion and approval."

9. 25 U.S.C. §465.

10. 25 C.F.R. §1.4.

11. Chapman v. Houston Welfare Rights Organization, 441 U.S. 600, 613 (1979).

12. U.S. Const., Art. VI, §2.

13. Village of Hobart's Response to Plaintiff's Motion to Strike Affirmative Defenses and Dismiss Counterclaims.

14. 555 U.S. 379 (2009).

15. Village of Hobart's Answer, Affirmative Defenses and Counterclaim.

16. 25 C.F.R. §1.4.

17. Village of Hobart's Third-Party Complaint for Declaratory, Injunctive, and Monetary Relief, 14. Oneida Tribe of Indians of Wisconsin v. Village of Hobart, 891 F.Supp.2d 1058, 1071 (E.D. Wis. 2012).

18. Treaty with the Oneida, 7 Stat. 566, February 3, 1838, Article 2.

19. Village of Hobart's Third-Party Complaint for Declaratory, Injunctive, and Monetary Relief, Citing Clean Water Act, 33 U.S.C. 1342(p), and Wis. Stat. §283.33(1)(c).

20. Oneida Tribe of Indians of Wisconsin v. Village of Hobart, 891 F.Supp.2d 1058, 1071 (E.D. Wis. 2012).

21. Oneida Tribe of Indians of Wisconsin v. Village of Hobart, 891 F.Supp.2d 1058, 1071 (E.D. Wis. 2012).

22. Oneida Tribe of Indians of Wisconsin v. Village of Hobart, 732 F.3d 837, 842 (7th Cir. 2013).

23. March 2013 Letter from Richard R Heidel, Village President, to "Hobart Friends, Neighbors, and Constituents." Copy on file with author. Emphasis in original.

24. Transcribed from audio recording of the oral arguments, accessed February 24, 2021, https://media.ca7.uscourts.gov/sound/2013/sp.12-3419.12-3419_09_18_2013.mp3.

25. This latter incident is referenced in the Nation's resolution concerning government-to-government relations with the Village. BC Resolution 2-20-08-C.

———— ✧ ————

CHAPTER 8

The Big Apple Fest Case

The Village of Hobart's Failed Attempt to Put an End to the Oneida Reservation and Obtain Control over the Oneida Nation

JAMES R. BITTORF and ARLINDA F. LOCKLEAR

KEY TERMS IN THIS CHAPTER

- Indian Country
- Tribal sovereign immunity
- Treaty
- Allotment
- Fee patents
- Reservation diminishment/disestablishment
- Exceptional circumstances

The 1838 Treaty with the Oneida established the Oneida reservation. Within the boundaries of the reservation, the Oneida Nation exercises self-governance and is not subject to state or local regulation. This has long rankled the leadership of the Village of Hobart.

In 2016 the Village threatened to enforce its special-event ordinance against the Nation and its officials and employees if the Nation held its annual Big Apple Fest without first obtaining a village special-event permit. The Nation sued the Village in federal district court to prevent the Village from interfering with the event and to challenge the citation and the $5,000 fine issued by the Village to the Nation after the event. The Nation claimed the Village's attempts to enforce its ordinance were preempted by federal law for two reasons: (1) the Nation, its trust lands, and its reservation are subject to comprehensive and pervasive federal regulation that leaves no room for Village regulation; and (2) Village regulation would impermissibly interfere with the Nation's inherent powers of self-governance and sovereignty. In its answer, the Village claimed that (1) the Big Apple Fest did not occur within the boundaries of an existing Indian reservation; (2) the secretary of the interior lacks authority to re-move land from Village jurisdiction by taking it in trust; (3) the Nation was not under federal jurisdiction in 1934 when the Indian Reorganization Act was enacted and therefore is not eligible to have land taken into trust; and (4) the Village otherwise possesses jurisdiction to impose its ordinance on the Nation. The Village sought a declaration that it is entitled to enforce its ordinance against the Nation and a monetary judgment in the amount of the fine it levied against the Nation.

After lengthy discovery procedures and the exchange of expert historical reports, the district court ruled the Oneida reservation had been diminished through allotment and fee patenting and now consists only of lands held in trust, effectively reducing the reservation from 65,400 acres to roughly 14,000 acres.[1] The district court denied the Village's claim for a monetary judgment, however, on the ground it was barred by the Nation's sovereign immunity.[2] The Nation appealed the district court's ruling to the United States Court of Appeals for the Seventh Circuit, and the Seventh Circuit reversed. The Seventh Circuit observed that SCOTUS has "time and time again" rejected the claim that an Indian reservation may be disestablished or diminished through allotment and fee patenting.[3] The Seventh Circuit also dismissed the Village's supposedly unambiguous historical evidence as "so inconclusive that it could not justify a finding that the United States unilaterally broke the 1838 Treaty."[4] Finally, the Seventh Circuit ruled that no exceptional circumstances existed that might justify Village jurisdiction over the Nation.[5] In short, the Village lost resoundingly on both the facts and the law.

Background

The Village's Goal of Eliminating the Nation's Sovereignty

The Village has engaged in a long-term effort to undermine the Nation's sovereignty, eliminate the Nation's right to self-governance, and subject the Nation to the Village's laws. In 2008 the Village hired Elaine Willman as its director of development and tribal affairs. Willman had long advocated for the termination of tribal governments, which she equates with "tribalism": "What if tribalism were no longer an allowable form of government within the United States? . . . The loss of tribal governments would be deemed severe by corrupt tribal leaders, undoubtedly. Too bad."[6] She has framed the goal of eradicating tribal governments in stark, combative terms: "With the billions and blood we're spilling to free Middle-Eastern countries of tribal tyrannies, it is sheer insanity and unconscionable that tribalism as a form of government is simultaneously escalating across American lands. The United States was populated and created by people escaping monarchies and tribalism, and all the misery and inequality that go with them."[7]

Shortly after the Village hired Willman, Village president Richard Heidel confirmed that the Village Board largely shares her views: "When we met her face to face, she impressed us with her knowledge and credentials. . . . Where we (Hobart and Oneida) start to butt heads is when it leaves the realm of tribal culture and history and enters the realm of tribal government. . . . It's fair to say our board and Elaine's views with respect to tribal government are more alike than dissimilar. So call it a signal or an explicit statement, call it what you like."[8]

The Village later retained Willman as a "federal Indian policy consultant" to "act as an expert in federal Indian law and constitutional law."[9]

The Village faced a formidable obstacle in its effort to do away with the Nation's sovereignty: under federal law, all land within an Indian reservation is "Indian country," and within Indian country, state and local governments possess very limited jurisdiction over Indian tribes and their members. They may exercise such jurisdiction only when Congress has explicitly authorized them to do so or when exceptional circumstances exist that warrant setting aside the normal rules prohibiting state and local governments from interfering with tribal sovereignty and self-determination.[10] The Village therefore sought to disestablish the Nation's reservation and erase the Nation's Indian country in order to gain control over the Nation. With Willman's encouragement, the Village publicly challenged the existence of the Oneida reservation.[11] The Village also challenged the Nation's sovereignty and claimed, contrary to federal law, that it possessed jurisdiction over the Nation and tribal members on the reservation and that compliance with tribal law was not necessary. The Village Board declared:

> The Village enjoys local zoning, permitting, environmental and other controls on land owned in fee, regardless of the fact that it lies within a former Indian Reservation. If your property is taxable, it is fee land. For the most part, this is true whether the taxable (fee) land is owned by a tribal government, individual tribal member, or non-tribal member. . . .
>
> Consequently, with rare exception, those who own land in the Village are required to abide by Village ordinances, including but not limited to those dealing with zoning and permitting. Obtaining similar approval from the Tribe is not necessary.[12]

In the words of the Village president, the Village Board took "a proactive approach in educating other local governmental bodies about this FORMER Indian Reservation and about their own governmental authority and responsibilities."[13]

The Village also faced an obstacle in executing its plan. As a sovereign Indian tribe, the Nation possesses sovereign immunity from suit, and the Village could not sue the Nation to present its disestablishment claims in court. The Village therefore hoped to provoke a lawsuit from the Nation so that the Village could raise its disestablishment claims in its answer. Willman laid out this plan in an email that she shared with the Village Board in July of 2014:

> We're starting a deep dive, in a tiered/phased process that will ultimately challenge most of the existing trust parcels in Hobart, of the Oneidas. This will likely lead to a lawsuit filed against us by the Tribe, which we

welcome in order to get to two other pieces: 1) the disestablishment of the Reservation; and 2) the fact that this tribe is not eligible (under a 2009 Carcieri v. Salazar ruling) to have federal lands taken into trust. These are the BIG tickets that we're heading toward, going step-by-step, and based upon federal records we already have, and are accumulating.[14]

In November and December 2014 and March 2015, the Village Board took up "Reservation Status and Disestablishment Considerations" on its closed session tribal affairs agenda.[15] In August 2015, the Village chief of police advised the Nation that it must obtain a special-event permit for its annual Big Apple Fest or face "fines of up to $2,000 plus costs for each day of violation and each location in violation."[16] In response, the Nation informed the Village that the "Big Apple Fest is held within the Oneida Reservation boundaries and . . . is also taking place on a 'trust' parcel" and that the Village "lacks authority to require the Oneida Tribe to obtain permits for such activities."[17] The Nation held the event without a village permit, and the Village did not follow through on its threat.

In March 2016, the Village adopted an amended special-event ordinance that added a definition clarifying that "persons" subject to the ordinance include a "governmental entity, or organization of any kind."[18] In August of that year, the Village chief of police again advised the Nation that it must obtain a special-event permit for its annual Big Apple Fest,[19] and in September, the Village's attorney threatened to take enforcement action if the Nation did not obtain a permit and advised that the Nation's event coordinator and the Nation, "along with all responsible officials, will be cited pursuant to §1.3 of the Village Code, and will be subject to forfeitures of up to $10,000 for each violation, plus the cost of prosecution, as well as other potential penalties."[20]

In order to avoid Village interference with the Big Apple Fest, the Nation filed a lawsuit against the Village in federal district court seeking a declaration that the Nation is not subject to the Village's special-event ordinance and seeking an injunction prohibiting the Village from attempting to enforce its ordinance. The district court declined to issue a preliminary injunction when the Village agreed not to disrupt the event. After the Nation held the event without a permit, the Village issued a citation to the Nation seeking to impose a $5,000 fine. The Nation then filed an amended complaint recounting these events, and the Village filed an answer alleging, among other things, that the Big Apple Fest did not take place within the boundaries of an existing Indian reservation.

The Nation's Special Events

The Nation has a long and proud history of hosting public events and ceremonies that showcase its history, culture, and economy. The Nation's weekly farmer's market during the summer months features dozens of vendors, both Indian and non-Indian, with locally grown produce, crafts, and other goods for sale. The Nation's annual Pow-Wow, a community event for more than forty-five years, attracts up to twenty thousand attendees, hosts Native American dancers from around the country, and features Native American singers, foods, and crafts and Lacrosse exhibitions. Similarly, the Nation's annual Big Apple Fest, which takes place at the Nation's Apple Orchard and Cultural Heritage Grounds, offers tours of historic Oneida homes, apple picking, horse and wagon rides, demonstrations of Oneida crafts, a farmer's market, and family-oriented games and activities. Other annual events honor veterans, celebrate the Nation's on-reservation fishing rights, and bring families together for educational and recreational activities.

The Nation has always conducted these events and ceremonies under its own authority and under its own laws, without regulation by the state or local governments. The Nation's Tourism Division has expertise in the planning and production of large-scale community events that are safe and successful and coordinates with the Oneida Police Department, the Oneida Security Department, the Oneida Emergency Management Department, Oneida Risk Management, Oneida Environmental Health and Safety, the Oneida Comprehensive Health Division, and other departments and divisions of the Nation as necessary. Through its departments and divisions, the Nation enforces applicable laws at these events, including the Oneida Vendor Licensing Law, the Oneida Food Service Code, the Oneida On-Site Waste Disposal Ordinance, the Oneida Recycling and Solid Waste Disposal Law, the Oneida Safety Law, the

Oneida Sanitation Ordinance, and the Oneida Tribal Regulation of Domestic Animals Ordinance.

The Village's Special-Event Ordinance

The Village is a relative newcomer when it comes to regulating public events, having first enacted its special-event ordinance in 2014. As amended in 2016, the ordinance attempts to subject any person or entity holding a public event to oversight by the Village Board, which is responsible for administering the ordinance.[21] The ordinance also imposes a wide range of conditions on the issuance of permits, including liability insurance requirements, indemnification of the Village, requirements for written requests for Village services, mandatory use of the Village police department in the event security services are deemed necessary, cleaning and damage deposits, business licenses for vendors, and inspections.[22] The Village reserves the right to shut down an event "if it is deemed to be a public safety hazard . . . and/or there is a violation of Village ordinances, state statutes or the terms of the applicant's permit."[23] And the Village reserves the right to deny permit applications for a host of reasons.[24]

Litigation

On September 2, 2016, the Village's attorney wrote to the Nation's special events coordinator, who was at the time in the final planning stages for the 2016 Big Apple Fest, scheduled to take place on September 17. The letter advised that the Nation must apply for a permit from the Village under the Village's special-event ordinance no later than September 9. Further, the letter advised that, in the event the Nation failed to do so, the Nation and all "responsible officials" would be prosecuted for violation of the ordinance.[25]

Proceedings in the District Court

The Nation did not apply for a permit from the Village. Instead, the Nation filed a lawsuit against the Village in federal district court, seeking a declaration that the Nation and its officials are immune from the Village's ordinance within the boundaries of the reservation.[26] At the same time, the Nation asked the court to stop the Village from making any effort to enforce its ordinance against the Nation or the Nation's officials or otherwise interfere with the Big Apple Fest.[27] The district court conducted a hearing on the Nation's request for an injunction and, relying on the Village's representation that it would not interfere with the event, denied the request.[28] The Big Apple Fest took place as planned on September 17 without incident. On September 21, the Village chief of police issued a citation to the Nation for refusing to apply for a Village permit and demanded payment of a $5,000 fine. The Nation then amended its complaint, seeking a declaration that the Nation and its officials are immune from the ordinance and the fine imposed by the Village.[29]

In both its original and its amended complaint, the Nation made two claims. First, the Nation asserted that federal law prohibited the application of the Village's ordinance to the Nation with respect to activity on its lands and within the boundaries of its reservation, as established by the 1838 Treaty with the Oneida.[30] Second, the Nation asserted that it has the inherent power of self-government to manage its lands and activities within the boundaries of the reservation and that the imposition of the Village's ordinance infringed on these inherent powers of sovereignty. The Nation sought a declaration that the Village lacked authority to impose its ordinance on the Nation and a permanent injunction against the Village's attempts to do so.

The Village filed an answer and asserted several claims against the Nation. The Village admitted attempting to impose its ordinance on the Nation, including issuing a citation for the Nation's alleged violation of the ordinance, but denied that the Nation is immune from the ordinance. The Village's major contentions were stated in its own claims, including: the Big Apple Fest did not take place within the boundaries of an existing Indian reservation; the Nation is not eligible for land-into-trust under the Indian Reorganization Act (IRA), the federal statute which authorizes the Secretary of the Interior to accept land into trust for tribes; and the circumstances of the Big Apple Fest were such that it justified an exception to the Nation's usual immunity, even if the reservation continued to exist.[31]

The Nation's complaint and the Village's answer and other documents filed in the case made clear that the dispute depended upon the court's interpretation of the 1838 Treaty and certain federal statutes. The legal standards governing the construction of the Treaty and federal statutes are clear. First, treaties with tribes are to be interpreted as the parties understood them at the time, and any ambiguities are to be resolved in favor of the tribe.[32] If the United States and the Oneida Nation understood the 1838 Treaty to create a reservation, then that understanding is binding on the court. Second, once created, an Indian reservation continues to exist unless and until the United States Congress acts to either diminish the size of the reservation or abolish it altogether.[33] Finally, Congress has by statute defined all land within the boundaries of a reservation, including fee parcels, to be "Indian country" for jurisdictional purposes.[34]

Both the Nation and the United States have consistently interpreted the 1838 Treaty as establishing the Oneida reservation for the Nation. The State of Wisconsin and local municipal governments other than the Village share this view.[35] All Congress had done regarding the reservation after 1838 was to authorize the allotment of the reservation under the General Allotment Act of 1887 (GAA) and to authorize the early issuance of fee patents to Oneida allottees before the expiration of the usual twenty-five-year trust period in a 1906 act.[36] Although courts have consistently ruled that allotment under the GAA and the issuance of fee patents does not abolish or alter the boundaries of an Indian reservation,[37] the Village nonetheless claimed the allotment of the Oneida reservation and the issuance of fee patents on the reservation disestablished or diminished the reservation. The Village also claimed the Nation was bound by the cursory analysis in a 1933 federal court decision that stated the reservation had been discontinued.[38]

The Nation and the Village had very different ideas about how the lawsuit should proceed. On November 14, 2016, the Village served a wide-ranging discovery request on the Nation, seeking documents from the Nation on the entire history of its relationship with the United States, the acquisition of every parcel acquired in trust by the United States for the Nation under the IRA, the creation and subsequent history of the Oneida reservation, and every aspect of the 2016 Big Apple Fest. The Village also sought a long delay on all proceedings while it engaged in this extensive discovery. On the other hand, the Nation moved for summary judgment, arguing that, under the governing legal standards, all issues could be resolved in the Nation's favor simply by applying the terms of the Treaty of 1838, the GAA, the 1906 act, the IRA, and the Indian country statute. Finally, the Nation argued that the Village had not identified any exceptional circumstances that might support imposition of its ordinance on the Nation on the reservation.[39]

The Nation and the Village filed competing motions in which the Nation sought to cut off or limit discovery and the Village sought expansive discovery. The district court took a middle ground. It allowed discovery to take place and, as a result, denied the Nation's motion for summary judgment. But it did not allow the expansive discovery sought by the Village and refused to reconsider the Nation's status as federally recognized or to require that the Nation provide records on the history of every trust parcel on the reservation. As a practical matter, the district court limited discovery to the Village's arguments regarding the Treaty of 1838, whether the reservation had been disestablished or diminished, and whether exceptional circumstances justified Village regulation of the Big Apple Fest. Even so, this discovery took eighteen months to complete and included the exchange of thousands of pages of documents, the preparation and exchange of four expert historian reports (three for the Nation and one for the Village), the depositions of the four experts, and the depositions of more than a dozen officials from the Nation and the Village. The record was, indeed, full.

Upon completion of discovery, the Nation and the Village filed cross-motions for summary judgment. While the motions were supported by references to the very substantial record in the case, the arguments on the legal issues were the same as those identified early in the litigation. In the meantime, the United States decided to appear as *amicus curiae* in support of the Nation's position that the Oneida reservation, created by the Treaty of 1838, had never been disestablished or diminished by Congress.[40]

The District Court's Decision

The district court ruled against the Nation on the question of diminishment of the reservation and determined that the Village could impose its ordinance on the Nation on fee land. In its complicated decision, the district court held that (1) the Treaty of 1838 created the Oneida reservation for the Nation, and the Village lacked authority to regulate the activities of the Nation on the reservation to the extent that it had not been disestablished or diminished by Congress; (2) the allotment of the reservation under the GAA did not disestablish the reservation; (3) the issuance of fee patents on the reservation diminished the reservation, and the present-day reservation consists only of land held in trust by the United State; (4) the Village lacks authority to regulate the Nation on trust land; (5) the 1933 federal court decision was not binding on the Nation; and (6) the Nation's sovereign immunity barred the Village's attempt to collect its $5,000 fine. In the meantime, two other Apple Fests had taken place, and the Village had issued two more citations because of the Nation's continuing refusal to apply for a Village permit. All proceedings on these citations in the Village's municipal court were stayed, pending the final resolution of the federal lawsuit.

Proceedings in the Seventh Circuit

The Nation appealed the district court's decision to the United States Court of Appeals for the Seventh Circuit. Significantly, the Village did not cross-appeal on any issues—not on the determination that the Treaty of 1838 created a reservation, not on the conclusion that the Nation was not bound by the 1933 federal court decision, not on the finding that the Nation was immune from Village regulation on its trust lands (the "diminished Reservation"), and not on the ruling that the Nation was immune from Village's attempts to collect its $5,000 fine. By failing to cross-appeal the treaty-interpretation issue, the Village effectively abandoned its nonsensical reading of the 1838 Treaty.

In its opening brief, the Nation focused on the district court's analysis regarding the diminishment issue and demonstrated that the district court's conclusion directly contradicted a substantial body of Supreme

Court authority. The Nation also noted that the Village had abandoned its claim of exceptional circumstances to justify its regulation of the Nation's activities on the "diminished Reservation," its reliance on the 1933 federal court decision, and its ability to collect on the $5,000 fine.[41] The United States and the State of Wisconsin joined the Nation in defending the Oneida reservation, and filed *amicus curiae* briefs expressing the view that the boundaries of the Oneida reservation, as established under the Treaty of 1838, remained intact.[42] The National Congress of American Indians, the largest national organization representing the interests of Indian tribes, and the Indian Land Tenure Foundation, also filed an *amicus curiae* brief in support of the Nation, and argued that the diminishment standard used by the district court directly contradicted the standard set by SCOTUS and, if adopted, would call into question the status of literally dozens of Indian reservations which had been allotted under the GAA.[43]

In its response brief, the Village, remarkably, led with its insistence that the Nation was barred from defending the reservation because of the 1933 district court decision, even though the Village had not cross-appealed on the issue. On the principal issue of the status of the reservation, the Village did not resurrect its claim that the reservation had been disestablished altogether, but vigorously defended the district court's conclusion that the reservation had been diminished over time as fee patents were issued. Finally, the Village made a half-hearted attempt to demonstrate that exceptional circumstances justified its regulation of the Nation on the "diminished Reservation," and asked the Seventh Circuit to remand the case to the district court for further consideration of that issue.[44]

In its reply brief, the Nation's principal argument was that the governing standard under a large body of Supreme Court authority compelled the conclusion that the reservation had not been diminished, because there was no indication of congressional intent to diminish the reservation in the statutory text of either the GAA or the 1906 act. In addition, the Nation argued it was not bound by the 1933 district court decision since it was not a party to that case. Finally, the Nation vigorously disputed the idea that further consideration of the Village's claim of exceptional circumstances was necessary, as the parties had already engaged in massive discovery on the issue and fully briefed the issue, and the Village had lost and had failed to file a cross-appeal. In the Nation's view, the only issue before the Seventh Circuit was the district court's conclusion that the reservation had been diminished.

A three-judge panel of the Seventh Circuit heard oral arguments on the Nation's appeal by telephone conference call, in accordance with Covid-19 pandemic protocols. It was clear during the argument that the judges were not impressed with the Village's insistence that the 1933 federal court decision prevented the Nation from defending the reservation. Instead, the judges wanted to focus on the law and history regarding the claimed diminishment of the reservation. On this issue, two of the three judges expressed open skepticism about the Village's argument that scattered references in the historical record to the "former" reservation could accomplish diminishment of the reservation without a clear indication from Congress that it intended to alter the reservation's boundaries.

One question at oral argument did suggest how the Seventh Circuit might proceed. At the time of the argument, the case *McGirt v. Oklahoma* was pending before SCOTUS. One of the judges asked whether *McGirt* might impact Oneida and whether the panel should wait for SCOTUS's ruling in that case. The Nation's position was that the panel need not wait as *McGirt* did not involve the GAA and instead involved treaties and statutes that were unique to Indian territory in Oklahoma. Even so, the panel did wait for the decision in *McGirt*. Although the GAA was not at issue in that case, SCOTUS did review the general allotment policy and its impact on reservation boundaries. Specifically, SCOTUS indicated that, while the GAA created conditions for disestablishment, it did not legislate disestablishment.[45] And SCOTUS held that the State of Oklahoma was mistaken that reservation boundaries could be altered by historical circumstances, independent of statutory text indicating a congressional intent to do so.[46] The Nation immediately brought SCOTUS's analysis to the Seventh Circuit's attention.

The Seventh Circuit's Decision

The Seventh Circuit reversed the district court's ruling that the Oneida reservation had been diminished.[47] The Seventh Circuit reasoned that allotment alone, including the issuance of fee patents, did not alter reservation boundaries and addressed SCOTUS's decision in *McGirt* in relation to the established standard for deciding reservation disestablishment and diminishment claims. In summary, it held:

> We read *McGirt* as adjusting the *Solem* framework to place a greater focus on statutory text, making it even more difficult to establish the requisite congressional intent to disestablish or diminish a Reservation. The Oneida Nation prevails under the both the *Solem* framework and the adjustments made in *McGirt*. . . .
>
> *McGirt's* allotment analysis has turned what was a losing position for the Village into a nearly frivolous one. *McGirt* teaches that neither allotment nor the general expectations of Congress are enough to diminish a Reservation. The Village has no argument for diminishment grounded in statutory text. The statutes on which it relies only allow for the allotment of the Oneida Reservation or speed along the allotment process. No statutory text comes close to creating ambiguity regarding diminishment of Reservation boundaries.[48]

The Seventh Circuit also rejected the Village's reliance on the 1933 federal court decision, reasoning that the Nation was not a party and was not represented in that case.[49] Finally, the Seventh Circuit rejected the Village's exceptional-circumstances argument, finding that most of the Village's arguments had not been properly raised and that the one legal argument it made—that tribes have no immunity from local land use regulations as applied to fee land—was clearly wrong.[50]

The Village petitioned for rehearing by the same three-judge panel. Interestingly, the Village did not seek review by all the judges on the Seventh Circuit and effectively conceded that its petition did not present an important issue or a conflict with another circuit court of appeals or a decision of SCOTUS. Instead, the Village merely sought a remand to the district court for further consideration of its exceptional-circumstances claim. The panel denied the petition for rehearing, and at that point the countdown began for the Village to request that SCOTUS review the Seventh Circuit's decision. The clock ran out in February 2021. The Village did not seek review, and the decision is now final.

CLOSING OBSERVATIONS

The Seventh Circuit's decision in the Big Apple Fest case should mark a turning point in relations between the Nation and the Village. The Village has now lost all its major arguments against the Nation's sovereignty on its reservation. It has now been resolved that (1) the Treaty of 1838 created an Indian reservation for the Nation; (2) the reservation has never been diminished or disestablished; (3) the Nation is not bound by statements in old decisions about the reservation's status; (4) the Nation is organized under the IRA and qualifies for the land-into-trust process established in the IRA; and (5) exceptional circumstances will rarely if ever justify Village regulation of the Nation on its reservation. The Village raised all these issues and lost them all, once and for all time, in the Big Apple Fest case. Relations between the Nation and the Village can now be written on a clean slate, one not sullied by the Village's ideology, selective reading of history, and upside-down legal theories. This presents an opportunity for the Nation and the Village to forge a new relationship— a government-to-government relationship built upon mutual respect and the shared interests in good governance of their overlapping territory and the welfare of their constituents. We can hope that the Village will engage in sober reflection and seize this opportunity.

NOTES

1. Oneida Nation v. Village of Hobart, 371 F. Supp. 3d 500, 503, 515 (2019), *rev'd* 968 F.3d 664 (7th Cir. 2020).

2. Oneida Nation v. Village of Hobart, 371 F. Supp. 3d 500, 503, 515 (2019), *rev'd* 968 F.3d 664 (7th Cir. 2020), at 523.

3. Oneida Nation v. Village of Hobart, 968 F.3d 664, 668 (7th Cir. 2020).

4. Oneida Nation v. Village of Hobart, 968 F.3d 664, 668 (7th Cir. 2020).

5. Oneida Nation v. Village of Hobart, 968 F.3d 664, 668 (7th Cir. 2020).

6. Elaine Willman, *Impact of Federal Government Indian Policy upon the Fabric of American Government*, 2003, formerly available at http://www.parrı.com/ElaineWillman/Impact%20°f%20Federal%20Indian%20Policy% 20Upon%20 ther%20Fabric%20°f%20American%20Government.htm).

7. Elaine Willman, *Going to Pieces: The Dismantling of the United States of America*. Toppenish, WA, published by the author, 2005, 25.

8. "Official's Former Ties Seem Cause for Concern" (editorial), *Green Bay Press-Gazette*, January 10, 2008.

9. An Agreement for Consulting Services by and between the Village of Hobart, Wisconsin, and Consultant Elaine D. Willman of the Willman-Davis Intergovernmental Resource Services, June 16, 2015. Willman is not an attorney and is not licensed to practice law.

10. California v. Cabazon Band of Mission Indians, 480 U.S. 202 (1987).

11. Email from Elaine Willman to Village Board members ("if you read this case and substitute 'Oneida Tribe of Indians' for 'Stockbridge-Munsee'—it becomes very probable that THIS Reservation was long ago disestablished"), April 23, 2008; Richard Heidel, "From the Village President," *The Press*, Hobart Section, October 24, 2008, 22 ("It is the village's position the Oneida Reservation has been disestablished or diminished.").

12. "An Open Letter to Village of Hobart Property Owners" (paid advertisement), *The Press*, Hobart Section, September 11, 2009, 20.

13. Prepared Remarks of Richard Heidel, CERA Conference Presentation, Washington, D.C., November 16, 2015.

14. Email from Elaine Willman to Village Board members, July 7, 2014. Village president Heidel testified under oath at his deposition that the Village did not have a plan to challenge the reservation, that the existence of the reservation was "nothing that the Village of Hobart itself has raised as an issue or introduced as an issue" in the lawsuit, and that disestablishment of the reservation "has always been a topic of discussion," but the Village "never tried to contrive any set of circumstances to bring that about." Deposition of Richard R. Heidel, March 8, 2018, 54–55, 64, 103, 105.

15. Village of Hobart, Closed Session Tribal Affairs Agenda, November 18, 2014; Village of Hobart Closed Session Tribal Affairs Agenda, December 15, 2014; Village of Hobart Closed Session Tribal Affairs Agenda, March 3, 2015.

16. Email from Chief of Police Randy Bani to Attorney Rebecca Webster, August 27, 2015.

17. Letter from Chairwoman Cristina Danforth to Village president Richard Heidel, September 3, 2015.

18. Village of Hobart Municipal Code, §250-5, as amended.

19. Email from Chief of Police Randy Bani to Special Events Coordinator Richard Figuero, August 18, 2016.

20. Letter from Attorney Frank Kowalkowski to Oneida Special Events Coordinator Richard Figuero, September 2, 2016.

21. Village of Hobart Municipal Code, §250-4.

22. Village of Hobart Municipal Code, §250-7(A)-(H).

23. Village of Hobart Municipal Code, §250-7(G).

24. Village of Hobart Municipal Code, §250-8(A)-(M).

25. Letter from Attorney Frank Kowalkowski to Oneida Special Events Coordinator Richard Figuero, September 2, 2016.

26. Complaint for Declaratory and Injunctive Relief, Oneida Nation v. Vill. of Hobart, Case No. 16-CV-1217, Doc. 1 (E.D. Wis.).

27. Motion for Preliminary Injunction, Oneida Nation v. Vill. of Hobart, Case No. 16-CV-1217, Doc. 2 (E.D. Wis.).

28. Telephone Conference (Motion for Preliminary Injunction), Oneida Nation v. Vill. of Hobart, Case No. 16-CV-1217, Doc. 9 (E.D. Wis.).

29. First Amended Complaint, Oneida Nation v. Vill. of Hobart, Case No. 16-CV-1217, Doc. 10 (E.D. Wis.).

30. 7 Statutes at Large 566.

31. Defendant's Answer and Affirmative Defenses, Oneida Nation v. Vill. of Hobart, Case No. 16-CV-1217, Doc. 12 (E.D. Wis.).

32. Minnesota v. Mille Lacs Band of Chippewa Indians, 526 U.S. 172 (1999).

33. Nebraska v. Parker, 577 U.S. 481 (2016); Solem v. Bartlett, 465 U.S. 463 (1984).

34. 18 U.S.C. §1151(a). This statute is commonly referred to as the "Indian country statute" and has long been used by SCOTUS to decide jurisdictional questions. See, e.g., Solem v. Bartlett, 465 U.S. 463, 465 (1984).

35. The Village claimed the 1838 Treaty called for individual one-hundred-acre allotments and did not create a reservation, despite the fact the reservation was surveyed, mapped, and reserved from the public domain as one parcel containing 65,400 acres. For more on the Village's ahistorical reading of the Treaty, see chap. 2.

36. Act of February 8, 1887, 24 Stat. 388; Act of June 21, 1906, 34 Stat. 325, 380.

37. Mattz v. Arnette, 412 U.S. 481 (1973); Seymour v. Superintendent, 368 U.S. 351 (1962).

38. Defendant's Memorandum of Law in Support of Motion for Summary Judgment, Oneida Nation v. Vill. of Hobart, Case No. 16-CV-1217, Doc. 94 (E.D. Wis.).

39. See California v. Cabazon Band of Mission Indians, 480 U.S. 202 (1987).

40. *Amicus Curiae* Brief of United States, Oneida Nation v. Vill. of Hobart, Case No. 16-CV-1217, Doc. 126 (E.D. Wis.).

41. Brief and Appendix of Plaintiff-Appellant Oneida Nation, Oneida Nation v. Vill. of Hobart, App. No. 19-1981, Doc. 18 (7th Cir.).

42. *Amicus Curiae* Brief of United States, Oneida Nation v. Vill. of Hobart, App. No. 19-1981, Doc. 21 (7th Cir.); *Amicus Curiae* Brief of State of Wisconsin, Oneida Nation v. Vill. of Hobart, App. No. 19-1981, Doc. 31 (7th Cir.).

43. *Amicus Curiae* Brief of NCAI and ILTF, Oneida Nation v. Vill. of Hobart, App. No. 19-1981, Doc. 30 (7th Cir.).

44. Brief of Defendant-Appellee Village of Hobart, Oneida Nation v. Vill. of Hobart, App. No. 19-1981, Doc. 40 (7th Cir.).

45. McGirt v. Oklahoma, 591 U.S. ___, 140 S. Ct. 2452, 2465 (2020).

46. McGirt v. Oklahoma, 591 U.S. ___, 140 S. Ct. 2452 (2020) at 2468–69.

47. Oneida Nation v. Vill. of Hobart, 968 F.3d 667 (7th Cir. 2020).

48. Oneida Nation v. Vill. of Hobart, 968 F.3d 667 (7th Cir. 2020), at 685, 668.

49. Oneida Nation v. Vill. of Hobart, 968 F.3d 667 (7th Cir. 2020), at 688.

50. Oneida Nation v. Vill. of Hobart, 968 F.3d 667 (7th Cir. 2020), at 689.

CHAPTER 9

Rebuilding the Nation's Land Base, One Fee-to-Trust Application at a Time

REBECCA M. WEBSTER

KEY TERMS IN THIS CHAPTER

- Fee-to-trust
- Under federal jurisdiction
- Reservation diminishment/disestablishment

A variety of individuals and entities hold title to land on Indian reservations. Non-Indians can own land, state and local governments can own land, the federal government can own land, churches and nonprofits can own land, tribal citizens can own land, and tribal governments can own land. To further complicate this mix, land held by tribes and tribal citizens can be in fee status or in trust status. This mix of ownership is the direct result of federal Indian policy that removed tribes westward, placed them on reservations, eventually gave ownership of plots of reservation land to individual tribal members, and, more recently, provided a process to restore land to the status it had under federal treaties. Recall that in one generation the Oneida people lost ownership of roughly 90 percent of the land on the reservation through the policy of allotment.[1]

Congress embraced the policy of restoring land to tribal ownership and trust status in the Indian Reorganization Act (IRA) of 1934.[2] In the IRA, Congress recognized that previous federal policies geared toward assimilating tribal members into mainstream society had failed. In short, the IRA was intended to place the management of tribal affairs back in the hands of tribal governments and to restore tribal ownership of reservation lands. One mechanism to do this was the fee-to-trust process.[3] Within the IRA, Congress established a process for tribes to rebuild their land bases.

In 2010 and 2011, the Village of Hobart filed appeals of Bureau of Indian Affairs' decisions to take land into trust for the Nation. As with all these lawsuits, the Village centered the issue on itself and portrayed itself as a victim of the Nation's progress. Unlike the other cases, this series of cases is still pending, and the Nation is still awaiting final decisions. The Nation hopes the clarifications offered in the Big Apple Fest case described in chapter 8 will pave the way for a favorable decision in this series of fee-to-trust appeals.

BACKGROUND

Before getting into the details about this legal confrontation, it is important to revisit a bit of the history of the land on the Oneida reservation and to understand the complexities involved with the fee-to-trust process. The Oneida Nation has had a continuing relationship with the United States since at least 1784, when the Nation and other Haudenosaunee tribes entered into the Treaty of Fort Stanwix.[4] Ten years later, in 1794, the Haudenosaunee entered into another treaty with the United States, known as the Treaty of Canandaigua. This treaty established peace between the Haudenosaunee and the United States, secured land rights for the Haudenosaunee, and guaranteed annuity payments to the Haudenosaunee. In fact, the Oneida Nation still receives annual payments under this treaty to this day.

In the early 1820s, many Oneida people migrated to what would later become the State of Wisconsin.[5] A number of factors influenced the decision to move, including a fear of the United States' removal policy, vast loss of land due to treaties with New York, scarcity of timber, loss of resources, the desire to escape the hostile climate caused by the Revolutionary War and rampant racial strife, and the desire to prevent cultural changes. In 1838, ten years before Wisconsin gained statehood, the tribe entered into a treaty with the United States to forever reserve 65,400 acres of land for the use and occupancy of the Oneida people.[6] Less than fifty years later, in 1887, Congress passed the General Allotment Act, which was the result of a compromise between legislators who were motivated by the plight of Indians on reservations and others who wanted to get rid of reservations and get their hands on the land.[7] Congress recognized that tribal economy, culture, and religion were inherently tied to the tribal land base. Tribal lands were parceled out to individual Indians, who then received trust patents and subsequently fee title to the land. With few exceptions, this land became taxable within a few decades. Through tax foreclosures, mortgage foreclosures, and predatory acquisitions, the Oneida people lost title to much of the land on the Oneida reservation. Although allotment did not disestablish or diminish reservations, it had devastating effects on tribal land ownership and Indian communities. As a result of allotment and fee patenting, in one generation the Oneida people lost ownership of approximately 90 percent of the land on the Oneida reservation.[8]

In a change of federal policy toward Indians, Congress passed the Indian Reorganization Act in 1934, in part to help rebuild land bases decimated under the prior policy of allotment.[9] That same year, the Nation voted to accept application of the IRA. In November 1936 the Nation adopted a constitution under the IRA, and it was approved by the secretary of the interior in December of that year. The Nation's leaders were aware the IRA provided for the establishment of tribal corporations and hoped to get a jump on the process by establishing a tribal corporation under state law. Ultimately the Department of the Interior informed them that the IRA called for corporate charters issued by the federal government and that the corporation formed under state law was not the equivalent. In 1937, the secretary issued a corporate charter under federal law.

Also, in 1937, the Nation and the United States began to reacquire title to land on the Oneida reservation in trust for the Nation. In 1947, the United States Indian Service issued a report titled "Ten Years of Government under I.R.A.," written by Theodore Haas, chief counsel for the Indian Service.[10] This report would later be known as the Haas

Report and contained a listing of the tribes organized under the IRA, including the Oneida in Wisconsin.

FEE-TO-TRUST PROCESS

The process of having land taken into trust is complex, consists of a number of steps, and can span many years. It begins when the Nation files an application for land it previously purchased on the open market. That land is held in "fee" status. This means the land is taxable and the Nation holds the title to the land. When the federal government takes land into "trust" status, the Nation gives title to the land to the United States. The land is no longer taxable, and the United States holds title to the land in trust for the Nation.

All fee-to-trust applications contain an Oneida Business Committee resolution authorizing the land to be transferred into trust status, a warranty deed prepared for the secretary of the interior's signature, a title commitment, maps/surveys of the property, the statutory authority to take the land into trust, the reason the Nation is requesting to have the land taken into trust, the historical and proposed use of the land, tax information relating to the impact of removing the property from the tax rolls, identification of jurisdictional problems that may arise from the trust acquisition and proposed resolutions to any conflicts, identification of the additional responsibilities the BIA will incur as a result of the acquisition, and background environmental data. The Nation also sends consultation letters to the municipality, county, and state governments in whose jurisdiction the property is located. The letters identify the location of the property and the current use of the property and ask the governments to send information directly to the BIA, with a copy to the Nation, pertaining to annual property taxes levied, impacts resulting from removal of the property from the tax rolls, any special assessments levied against the property, any government services provided by the governments, and any potential land use conflicts that may arise. The letters ask the governments to provide this information to the BIA, with a copy to the Nation, within thirty days.

The secretary considers the information provided in the Nation's fee-to-trust application and the information and comments provided by the municipality, the county, and the state. The secretary also considers any concerns noted on the title commitment or surveys. The secretary must also comply with the requirements of the National Environmental Policy Act in making a determination whether to accept the land into trust. The level of analysis required is generally dependent on whether the land acquisition could significantly affect the environment. The levels of analysis include a categorical exclusion determination, an environmental assessment, and/or an environmental impact statement. The secretary will not accept any property in trust if there are environmental concerns associated with the acquisition. After all comments have been received and reviewed, after all title and survey issues have been addressed, and after the secretary determines there are no environmental concerns associated with the trust acquisition, the secretary may issue a decision on whether to take the land into trust. If the secretary decides to take the land into trust, and once the timeline for an appeal has run or if the secretary's determination to take land into trust is upheld on appeal, the secretary signs the warranty deed and the property is placed into trust.

IMPACTS OF FEE-TO-TRUST ACQUISITIONS

Having land taken into trust has a number of benefits for the Nation. When land is taken into trust status, it is removed from the local tax rolls. In addition, the Nation receives technical expertise and legal protections from the Bureau of Indian Affairs regarding transactions involving the land, such as assistance with leases, mortgages, easements, as well as concerns about trespass and unauthorized wood cutting. The primary reasons to have land taken into trust are to restore its inalienable status, to revive the federal protection of title to the land, and to receive technical assistance offered for transactions involving trust land. When land is placed in trust status, the land cannot be sold, leased, or encumbered without tribal and Department of Interior approval. The fee-to-trust process creates a protected land base and provides a safe environment to nurture and promote Oneida culture, economy, health, and political infrastructure. Returning the land to its status as inalienable, to be held forever by the United States for the benefit of the

Nation, ensures that tribal investments within the Oneida reservation will never be lost.

When land is taken into trust status, it is removed from the tax rolls, so state and local governments lose any revenue they previously collected when the property was part of the tax base. In addition, local governments can no longer condemn the land or impose special assessments against the land. However, the Nation's intergovernmental agreements address these impacts.[11] These agreements generally compensate local governments for services provided to tribal trust property while also recognizing the services the Nation provides. The Nation is not just a common landowner. It provides services to tribal citizens, including health care, elder care, social services, housing, public works, waste and recycling pickup, and education. The Nation also provides services to all residents of the reservation, including police protection, parks and recreation areas, cultural events, libraries, hunting and fishing permits, environmental restoration, public transportation, and utility services. With respect to jurisdictional concerns, the service agreements address cooperative land use planning efforts and recognize limits on local civil regulatory authority.

FEE-TO-TRUST CONSORTIUM

In 2004 the Nation entered into a fee-to-trust consortium to redirect self-governance funds to pay for BIA staff to work on the backlog of its fee-to-trust applications. The Nation receives self-governance funds pursuant to an agreement under the Indian Self-Determination and Education Assistance Act of 1975.[12] That act established a framework for tribes to assume responsibility for administering programs, services, functions, and activities involving tribal citizens, lands, and resources. The Nation first entered into a self governance agreement in 1995.[13] Because the Nation administers programs previously administered by the federal government, the federal government transfers funds to the Nation to pay for them.

This consortium agreement was modeled after a consortium agreement in California. However, a United States Government Accountability Office report questioned that agreement because California tribes may have used gaming funds to pay for BIA staff and the consortium had the potential to create a risk of bias in favor of the consortium tribes. As a result, the Nation's consortium agreement uses only self-governance funds. The tribes that joined the consortium include Milles Lacs, Ho Chunk, and Shakope Mdewakanton. Under the consortium, the Nation has been able to implement the fee-to-trust process in a timelier manner.

Village Objects to Nation's Fee-to-Trust Applications

In 2007 an intergovernmental agreement between the Nation and the Village of Hobart was nearing the end of its term. Under the agreement, the Nation agreed to compensate the Village for services it provided to trust land and the Village agreed not to object to the Nation's applications to have land taken into trust status. Unfortunately, the Village breached the terms of the agreement by raising objections to several of the Nation's pending applications. In response, the Nation passed a resolution acknowledging the breach along with a number of other issues percolating between the governments. The resolution expresses the frustrations of the Nation's elected representatives in their attempts to interact with the Village on a government-to-government basis. The entirety of BC Resolution 2-20-08-C is as follows:

> Resolution Regarding Government-to-Government Relations with the Village of Hobart
>
> WHEREAS, the Oneida Tribe of Indians of Wisconsin is a federally recognized Indian government and a treaty Tribe organized under the laws of the United States of America; and
>
> WHEREAS, the Oneida General Tribal Council is the governing body of the Oneida Tribe of Indians of Wisconsin; and
>
> WHEREAS, the Oneida General Tribal Council has delegated the authorities of Article IV of the Oneida Tribal Constitution to the Oneida Business Committee; and
>
> WHEREAS, the Tribe maintains government-to-government relations with the United States of America, the State of Wisconsin, and other

state and local governments, and has entered into government-to-government agreements with the United States, the State of Wisconsin, and other state and local governments; and

WHEREAS, the Tribe, through its governmental operations and revenue-raising enterprises, provides employment for over 3,000 individuals, and thereby contributes substantially to the state and local economy, which in turn benefits both the state government and local governments; and

WHEREAS, the Tribe plays a vital role in delivering governmental services to tribal members and non-Indians, and under its Gaming Compact makes substantial annual payments to the State which fund state programs and services; and

WHEREAS, the United States of America holds title to land for the benefit of the Tribe, and such land is exempt from state and local taxation; and

WHEREAS, in the spirit of mutual cooperation and of its own free will, the Tribe generally pays for the value of services which are provided by local municipalities and which benefit tax-exempt tribal trust properties by entering into government-to-government service agreements with local municipalities; and

WHEREAS, service agreements recognize not only the value of services provided by the local municipalities, but also the value of services provided by the Tribe, and generally provide that local municipalities will not object to fee-to-trust applications submitted by the Tribe to the Bureau of Indian Affairs; and

WHEREAS, the Village of Hobart is located entirely within the boundaries of the Oneida Indian Reservation established pursuant to the 1838 Treaty with the Oneida, 7 Stat., 566, and

WHEREAS, the Tribe has attempted to maintain government-to-government relations with the Village of Hobart, and entered into a service agreement with the Village of Hobart in 2004; and

WHEREAS, in 2007, the Village of Hobart breached the terms of the service agreement by objecting to fee-to-trust applications submitted by the Tribe to the Bureau of Indian Affairs; and

WHEREAS, the Village of Hobart has recently asserted that it possesses the authority to condemn tribal property and to impose fees and assessments against the Tribe and tribal property, and the Village and the Tribe are in engaged in litigation regarding these issues; and

WHEREAS, the Village of Hobart has rebuffed efforts by the Tribe to resolve differences between the two governments through negotiation; and

WHEREAS, the Village Board President has made militaristic references in relation to the Tribe, and has claimed that federal agencies working with the Tribe were "Jack booting" over residents of the Village, and that the Village will be "the point man on the rifle squad"; and

WHEREAS, the Village Board President has expressed the sentiment that the Tribe may celebrate its culture and traditions, but that the Tribe should not be allowed to exercise self-governance or self-determination, and should instead fall under state jurisdiction and control; and

WHEREAS, the Village Board sponsored a forum on the Oneida Reservation at which the disestablishment of tribal governments was advocated; and

WHEREAS, the attitudes and opinions expressed by the Village Board harken back to the past assimilationist policies of the federal government which were abhorrently destructive to Indian tribal government, tribal culture and the well-being of tribal members, and have long since been repudiated; and

WHEREAS, the Village Board has paradoxically expressed the desire to enter into a new service agreement with the Tribe; and

WHEREAS, the Oneida Business Committee finds it unreasonable and counterproductive to engage in service agreement negotiations with any entity which seeks the subjugation and disestablishment of the Tribe's government;

NOW THEREFORE BE IT RESOLVED, that the Oneida Tribe of Indians of Wisconsin will not enter into service agreement negotiations with the Village of Hobart until such time as the Village Board formally recognizes the right of the Oneida Tribe to maintain its own government and exercise jurisdiction within its Reservation, and the

Village Board abandons assimilationist rhetoric and attempts to change federal Indian Policy to the detriment of the Oneida Tribe.

As has been demonstrated throughout this book, the Village has not shown any inclination to participate in government-to-government discussions or to restore government-to-government relationships with the Nation. Instead, in lawsuit after lawsuit, the Village continues to challenge the Nation's rights to govern and exercise jurisdiction. With respect to fee-to-trust, the Village's objections would soon be included among these lawsuits.

IBIA Fee-to-Trust Appeal

In 2010 and 2011, the Village filed a total of five consolidated appeals with the Interior Board of Indian Appeals (IBIA) challenging the Bureau of Indian Affairs' (BIA) decisions to take land into trust for the Nation.[14] The IBIA is a body that reviews decisions made by the regional director of the Midwest Area Office of the BIA involving Indian tribes or tribal citizens. The Village's appeals to the IBIA involved six fee-to-trust applications covering a total of approximately five hundred acres of land. If the Nation had been successful in having this land taken into trust, at the time of the appeal the Village would have lost a combined annual total of $36,148.88, which represents 1.4 percent of the Village's annual budget.[15] The minimal loss of tax revenue suggests these appeals are about more than money. The Village has since filed additional appeals challenging fee-to-trust decisions.

The Village's main legal and factual claims in its appeals were that (1) the Oneida reservation and the Oneida Nation ceased to exist prior to 1934 and the Nation was fraudulently recreated under the IRA; (2) the secretary of the interior cannot take land into trust for the Nation because the Nation was not under federal jurisdiction in 1934; and (3) the fee-to-trust process is unconstitutional.[16] The IBIA affirmed the regional director's conclusions that the Nation was under federal jurisdiction in 1934 and was therefore eligible to have land taken into trust.[17] The IBIA took note of the historical record, finding that the Nation voted to accept application of the IRA in 1934 and that the Nation was later listed in the Haas Report in 1947. The IBIA also confirmed that some land on the Oneida reservation had never lost its trust status. Last, the IBIA acknowledged the Nation's long, continuous history of dealing with the federal government dating to at least 1794. As a result, the IBIA found that the secretary had the authority to take land into trust for the Nation.

The IBIA declined to consider the Village's third argument regarding the constitutionality of the IRA because the IBIA lacks jurisdiction to rule on the constitutionality of federal statutes. However, the Village's constitutional theories, including its claim that Congress does not have authority to remove land from state jurisdiction or to restore or create tribal sovereignty over such land, have been rejected by every court that has considered them. The Village's pursuit of these discredited theories demonstrates the Village's overarching goal of changing federal Indian law in favor of municipal control.

In addition to the legal arguments the Village advanced, it also claimed the BIA had abused its discretion in considering the regulatory factors for fee-to-trust acquisitions and that the BIA was impermissibly biased against the Village because of the fee-to-trust consortium. The IBIA affirmed the BIA's assessment of the Nation's need for land, the Nation's use of the land, and the BIA's ability to handle additional responsibilities associated with the trust acquisition. However, the IBIA remanded the case back to the BIA for consideration of four issues: (1) loss of tax revenue; (2) jurisdictional and land use conflicts; (3) environmental concerns; and (4) the Village's claims of bias with respect to the fee-to-trust consortium. The IBIA concluded the regional director had not sufficiently addressed the first three issues, and the regional director had had no opportunity to address the fourth as the Village had raised its bias claims for the first time on appeal. The BIA resolved all four issues in favor of the Nation and issued new decisions to take land into trust for the Nation in 2017. The Village again appealed to the IBIA. The appeals have been fully briefed and are still awaiting IBIA decisions.

Closing Observations

The briefs the Village filed in its fee-to-trust appeals had blatantly racist undertones. The Village referred to Oneida Nation citizens as "Indians of Oneida Descent" in an attempt to racialize and delegitimize the status of the Nation and its citizens. Section 479 of the IRA addresses the definition for the term "Indian" to determine who is eligible to have land taken into trust: "The term 'Indian' as used in this Act shall include all persons of Indian descent who are members of any recognized Indian tribe now under Federal jurisdiction, and all persons who are descendants of such members who were, on June 1, 1934, residing within the present boundaries of any Indian reservation, and shall further include all other persons of one-half or more Indian blood."[18]

One of the factors the Nation pointed to when demonstrating that the Nation has been under federal jurisdiction since at least 1794 are the continued annuity payments the federal government still makes under the Treaty of Canandaigua. When discussing these annuity payments, the Village made blatantly racist comments in its brief. The Village insinuated that before they left New York, the Oneida people intermarried with non-Indians to such an extent that by the time the Oneidas reached what would later become Wisconsin, they lacked the blood quantum necessary to be considered Indian any more. The Village essentially said that Oneida people were not part of any tribal entity and were so white that we had to form a corporation to attempt to come within the terms of the IRA. The following is an excerpt from the Village's opening brief in the fee-to-trust appeals.

> Additionally, even if the Oneidas of Wisconsin are entitled to and are receiving annuity payments, that does not mean they were "Indians now under federal jurisdiction" pursuant to Sec. 479. The mere fact that the federal government could trace the ancestry, to owe someone money, does not mean that person was half-blood or more as of June 1, 1934. Because there was no existing tribal entity on June 1, 1934, the definition of Indian applies directly. The Oneida descendants were intermarried with whites before they ever left New York in 1838. If there had been a group of half bloods or more as of June 1934, it would have not been necessary to create a state tribal corporation to attempt to apply the IRA to these individuals.[19]

It's difficult to articulate how exhausting and infuriating it was to read the Village's briefs, hear its oral arguments, and sit in its meetings. The Village was persistent in asserting control over the narrative presented to the public by attempting to rewrite history and discount the validity of Oneida people, history, culture, and governance. I can only hope that this book will help tell the story from the perspective of the Oneida people.

NOTES

1. See chap. 2 for more information on the allotment acts.

2. 25 U.S.C. §461 et seq. (June 18, 1934). Renumbered as 25 U.S.C. §5108.

3. Some of the content in this chapter previously appeared in 2010 in a series of articles in the tribal newspaper *Kalihwisaks* (She Looks for News). The Oneida Law Office ran a series of articles to provide information to the Oneida community on a variety of land and intergovernmental relations issues. Copies of the newspaper editions with the articles related to fee-to-trust can be found at https://oneida-nsn.gov/wp-content/uploads/2017/11/02-February-4 -2010.pdf, https://oneida-nsn.gov/wp-content/uploads/2017/11/02-February-18 -2010.pdf, and https://oneida-nsn.gov/wp-content/uploads/2017/11/03-March -4-2010.pdf, all accessed June 3, 2021.

4. The tribes that constitute the Haudenosaunee Confederacy include the Mohawk, Seneca, Oneida, Cayuga, Onondaga, and Tuscarora.

5. See chap. 1 for further discussion on the removal of the Oneida people to what would later become the State of Wisconsin.

6. Treaty with the Oneida.

7. 25 U.S.C. ch. 9 §331 et seq., 25 U.S.C. ch. 9 §349.

8. A. Locklear, "The Allotment of the Oneida Reservation and Its Legal Ramifications," in *The Oneida Indian Experience*, ed. J. Campisi and L. M. Hauptman (New York: Syracuse University Press, 1988).

9. 25 U.S.C. §461 et seq.

10. Theodore H. Haas, "Ten Years of Tribal Government under I.R.A.," 1947, https://www.doi.gov/sites/doi.gov/files/migrated/library/internet/subject/up load/Haas-TenYears.pdf.

11. See chap. 5 for more discussion on intergovernmental agreements.

12. 25 U.S.C. ch. 14, subch. II §5301 et seq.

13. Oneida Business Committee Resolution 04-05-95C, April 5, 1995, https:// oneida-nsn.gov/wp-content/uploads/2016/02/04-05-95-C-Self-governance-com pact.pdf.

14. Hobart v. Midwest Regional Director, Bureau of Indian Affairs, 57 IBIA 4 (2013).

15. Village of Hobart's combined Reply Brief to Appellee's Brief and Oneida Tribe of Indians' Brief, 39. Hobart v. Midwest Regional Director, Bureau of Indian Affairs, 57 IBIA 4 (2013).

16. The Village pled these first two legal theories in other cases, most notably the Big Apple Fest Case. See chap. 8 for a discussion about the Big Apple Fest case.

17. Hobart v. Midwest Regional Director, Bureau of Indian Affairs, 57 IBIA 4 (2013).

18. 25 USC §479, renumbered 25 U.S. Code §5129.

19. Village of Hobart's Opening Brief, Hobart v. Midwest Regional Director, Bureau of Indian Affairs, 57 IBIA 4 (2013), 28.

Conclusion

"Dear Sir: I Am an Oneida Indian Living on the Reservation"

REBECCA M. WEBSTER

At this point, it's unclear what moves the Village will make next. I find it doubtful that the current Village Board will change tactics and begin to work cooperatively with the Nation. It may take a change in Village leadership, and that would take a change at the polls. Most often, incumbent Village Board members run unopposed. When the occasional candidate is either an Oneida Nation citizen or a non-Oneida candidate who runs on a platform of cooperation with the Nation, the candidate loses by a landslide. Until a majority of the voters decide they need a change, the Nation will likely stay the course.

Until we see a change in Village leadership, we will likely see a continued effort to erase Oneida governance and history and replace it with a whitewashed version of the Village's own history. One of the Village's opening briefs in its fee-to-trust appeals included correspondence between Oneida citizens and the federal government as "evidence" the Oneida reservation had been disestablished and that the Oneida Nation was not under federal jurisdiction in 1934. Among the exhibits were a number of letters involving my family members.[1] One in particular was from Henry "Duke" Doxtator, my maternal great-great-great grandfather.[2] He was a vocal critic of the allotting and fee patenting of reservation lands. He feared that the loss of the tribal land base would create beggars of tribal members. The letter he sent to the federal government is as follows:

Dear Sir:

I am an Oneida Indian living on the Reservation. I was introduced to you last fall by H. Jansen. I have never applied for neither do I want a patent in fee simple for my land. Am satisfied as it is. I wish you to inform me if my personal property is subject to taxation. Also if an act passed by Congress on Feb. 8th 1887 made Indians on Oneida Reservation citizens compulsory or otherwise I have never used the right of franchise and would like to have you inform me if I am not still a ward of the Government and exempt from personal property taxes. Thanking you in advance for any information that you can give me I remain

Respt

Henry Doxtator[3]

Duke received a response stating that his personal property was taxable. The Village used this letter and the federal government's response in an attempt to bolster its claim that the reservation had been disestablished. At the time, the law concerning taxation of personal property was not settled, but it is now well-established law that the personal property of tribal citizens on reservations is not subject to state or local taxation.[4] It is also now well settled that the Oneida reservation was not disestablished.

Duke's letter also holds another key piece of information that the Village omitted in its brief. His letter demonstrates how hard the Oneida people had been fighting to retain our sovereignty and our rights. The opening statement of his letter explains all we need to know about his perspective on the issue: "I am an Oneida Indian living on the Reservation."

Along similar lines, consider this revisionist narrative from the Village's website describing the history of the area:

Hobart's origins are rooted in the original Northwest Territory surrounding the Great Lakes. It is founded upon ancestral lands of the Menominee Indian tribe. While a Treaty of 1838 created a temporary reservation for then migrating Oneida tribal members from New York, the former reservation land was entirely ceded to the State of Wisconsin upon its statehood. In the late 1800s a majority vote of Wisconsin Oneida tribal members elected to have the reservation entirely allotted to individual tribal members through the Dawes Act of 1887.

Tribal members discovered during the allotment era that having land required roads, so from 1892 until 1908 Oneida tribal members pleaded with Brown and Outagamie county supervisors to establish and incorporate towns, so that municipal tax could be collected for the creation of roads and schools. In 1908, the Town of Hobart was created and became local authority. By the early 1900s numerous European settlers obtained land within the Town of Hobart, joining with Oneidas for the area's primary use of the land—farming.[5]

The Village and its allies like to rewrite current events as well. Consider the formation of the North East Wisconsin Citizens for Equal Rights (NEWCER), an offshoot of the Citizens Equal Rights Alliance (CERA), an antitropal organization that advocates for sweeping changes in federal Indian law in favor of state and municipal governments and against tribal sovereignty. Google "CERA" and "hate group" and you come up with some colorful hits. CERA's website lists our local organizations and their goals. Here is what they have listed for NEWCER:

NEWCER was formed for the purpose of educating the citizens of Northeast Wisconsin regarding tribal issues, to support our Village of Hobart elected officials and to work toward the equal rights of all citizens of Northeastern Wisconsin. We also saw the need to provide assistance to the Village of Hobart in its struggle to retain and maintain full municipal jurisdiction as the Tribal Government attempts to take over control.[6]

This last part of the statement, "as the Tribal Government attempts to take over control," is laughable at best. The Nation has never attempted to regulate outside its jurisdiction, unlike the Village, which has made repeated attempts to force the Nation to comply with Village ordinances. No amount of revising history or obfuscating current events can or should diminish the lessons we can learn from the recent interactions between the Village and the Nation. As promised in the introduction to this book, my research has offered recommendations for those tribal and local governments that want to increase positive intergovernmental relationships, especially when planning to utilize their shared spaces. My recommendations are as follows:

- Concentrate on strengthening interpersonal relationships among government officials and planners from the Tribe and local governments;
- Consider a more regional approach to planning practices, and engage neighboring governments to pool resources and work on more projects that benefit the entire community;
- Come to a common understanding concerning the jurisdictional limitations of tribal and local governments; and
- Find ways to learn about tribal and local government services in order to find equitable ways to acknowledge and compensate each other for providing those services.[7]

At the end of the day, if a local government is unable or unwilling to deal with the Nation on a government-to-government basis, the Oneida people consider the faces yet to be born. Despite our history of colonization, removal, and assimilation, we are still here, and we are thriving. We will continue to rebuild, knowing that we are making the way for future generations. Our ancestors had to lay down much of their identity just to survive. We are now picking that back up again. We are instilling our language, culture, history, and ceremonies in our youth. Every piece of land we purchase today is one they will not have to purchase tomorrow. Elected officials will come and go. Tribal, local, and federal policies shift with the wind. Our one constant is the need to do all we can so our future generations can not only continue to survive but continue to thrive—and to do so on our own terms in ways that make sense for us as Oneida people. We are on that path. We are in this for the long haul. The reservation is our home even though we may not all physically reside here. Speaking for those of us that do live here, I leave you with words fashioned from Henry "Duke" Doxtator: We are Oneida Indians living on the reservation.

Respectfully,

Kanyʌʔtake·lu / Rebecca M. Webster

Notes

1. See chap. 4 for more information about my family line.

2. The Village went out of its way to point out that he was from West DePere, a neighboring municipality. In fact, Duke was born and raised on the Oneida reservation and lived here his whole life. I also currently reside in this portion of the reservation and my mailing address is De Pere, even though I do not live in De Pere. We have this as our mailing address because that is the closest post office to our location on the reservation.

3. Hobart v. Midwest Regional Director, Bureau of Indian Affairs, 57 IBIA 4 (2013), Village of Hobart's Opening Brief, Exhibit 8.

4. Moe v. Salish & Kootenai Tribes, 425 U.S. 463, 48 L.Ed.2d 96, 96 S.Ct. 1634 (1976); Bryan v. Itasca County, 426 U.S. 373, 48 L.Ed.2d 710, 96 S.Ct. 2102 (1976); McClanahan v. Arizona Tax Commission, 411 U.S. 164, 36 L. Ed.2d 129, 93 S.Ct. 1257 (1973).

5. "Village Demographics," Village of Hobart, accessed June 9, 2021, https://www.hobart-wi.org/village-demographics. This narrative is also in the Village's 2014 annual budget: https://ecode360.com/documents/HO3209/pub lic/166812552.pdf, p. 15.

6. "Wisconsin Organizations," Citizens Equal Rights Alliance, accessed May 27, 2021, https://web.archive.org/web/20161225233822/http://citizensalliance.org/ wisconsin-organizations/.

7. R. M. Webster, "This Land Can Sustain Us: Cooperative Land Use Planning on the Oneida Reservation," *Planning Theory and Practice* 17, no. 1 (2016): 9–34, 30, doi: 10.1080/14649357.2015.1135250.

Glossary

Alienation: status of land that permits the owner of land to dispose of the property through a sale. In the case of Indian land title, alienation can also mean that an individual or tribe can also mortgage the land and grant easements or other rights in the land without the approval or consent of the federal government.

Allotment: a process through which the federal government transferred title to land on Indian reservations from the tribe (that held the land collectively for the benefit of all tribal members) to individual tribal members. Allotment transferred land from a traditional, communal system of land tenure to a government-imposed system of private landownership.

Condemnation/eminent domain: the taking of private property by a government entity for public use.

Exceptional circumstances: conditions required before a state or local government can grant itself additional powers.

Fee patents: documents issued by the federal government to individual tribal members after the expiration of the trust period under various federal allotment acts. When land gained fee status, owners of the land could mortgage or sell the land. The land also became taxable.

Fee-to-trust: a process available to tribes and tribal members who seek to have the United States take ownership of the land for the benefit of the tribe or tribal member. Land that goes into trust status is removed from the local tax rolls. Questions of jurisdiction on the land can also become clearer.

Home rule: a provision in a state's constitution that grants municipalities and/ or counties the right to pass laws to govern themselves as they see fit as long as those laws conform to state and federal constitutions. Under the Wisconsin constitution, cities and villages regulate matters that are of local concern. The legislature cannot enact laws that would preempt these local regulations unless the matter is of statewide concern or the law would apply uniformly to all cities and villages.

Indian Country: According to 18 U.S. Code §1151: "(a) all land within the limits of any Indian reservation under the jurisdiction of the United States Government, notwithstanding the issuance of any patent, and, including rights-of-way running through the reservation, (b) all dependent Indian communities within the borders of the United States whether within the original or subsequently acquired territory thereof, and whether within or without the limits of a state, and (c) all Indian allotments, the Indian titles to which have not been extinguished, including rights-of-way running through the same."

Intergovernmental agreement: a written agreement between two or more governments to cooperate to solve problems of mutual concern.

Real estate taxation: taxes levied against the land. Most common real estate taxes are property taxes that are based on the value of the property (ad valorem). However, there are other types of real estate taxes, such as taxes on the sale or transfer of the land, and property-related fees such as fees for water, sewer, refuse collection, stormwater, and ground water treatment.

Reservation diminishment/disestablishment: the legal process through which Congress reduces the size of a reservation (diminishment) or terminates the status of a reservation (disestablishment).

Restrictive covenants: a contractual agreement that imposes a restriction on the future use of land to preserve the value and peaceful enjoyment of neighboring land. In the case of the restrictive covenants at Thornberry creek (chapter 6), the restrictive covenant required the municipality to consent to the sale of the land if the sale would affect taxes or the municipal zoning jurisdiction.

Treaty: an agreement between a sovereign Indian nation and the United States government entered into between 1774 and 1871. Article Six of the United States Constitution holds that treaties "are the supreme law of the land."

Tribal sovereign immunity: the ability of a tribal government to regulate its internal affairs without being sued or brought before a court without its explicit consent.

Under federal jurisdiction: a status that requires the federal government to recognize its trust responsibility to an Indian tribe. The term is most relevant with respect to tribes that are eligible to have their lands taken into trust status regardless of whether that tribe was "under federal jurisdiction" when Congress passed the Indian Reorganization Act.

Zoning jurisdiction: the right of a government to require landowners to follow rules and regulations pertaining to acceptable land uses. Within reservation boundaries, municipal governments and tribal governments often have mixed jurisdiction over zoning matters. Determining which government has the final say over zoning matters can be a tricky task that can depend on factors such as who owns the land and whether the land is in trust status.

Index

Page numbers in *italic type* indicate illustrations.